Sailing with Columbus

The Arrival of Judaism in the Americas

ILEAN BALTODANO

Cover design idea by Gabriella Quitevis

PAGE PUBLISHING
Conneaut Lake, PA

First originally published by Page Publishing 2024

ISBN 979-8-89157-894-4 (pbk)
ISBN 979-8-89157-912-5 (digital)

Printed in the United States of America

Books by Ilean Baltodano

- *Still on Vacation (2017)*
- *Still on Vacation—In the Middle of a Pandemic—Revised (2019)*
- *Todavía de Vacaciones: En Medio de la Pandemia (2020) (Spanish translation)*
- *Sailing with Columbus: The Arrival of Judaism in the Americas (2024)*

To:

My mother,
for her love,
her energy,
strong work ethic, and
resourcefulness that drove
her entrepreneurial spirit.

My father,
who inspired me by
raising his voice for the voiceless
through his writings and poetry.

My daughters,
who are my motivation to not give up.

The survivors of the Holocaust,
their legacy should remain and remind us
that the Holocaust happened
and that we must fight for the helpless.

To deny people their human rights
is to
challenge their humanity.

—Nelson Mandela

Contents

Map of Mesopotamia

"The long history of the Jews began in Mesopotamia. Abraham was, basically, the father of the Jewish civilization. He was born in the Sumerian city—state of Ur around 2,000 BC. Sumerian was the earliest culture found in Mesopotamia."[1]

---

1   "What Is the Connection between Mesopotamia and Judaism?" https.//www. mometrix.com.

Map of Spain

"On March 31, 1492, in the Alhambra's resplendent Hall of the Ambassadors, Ferdinand and Isabella signed an edict, the Alhambra Decree, expelling the Jews from Spain."[2]

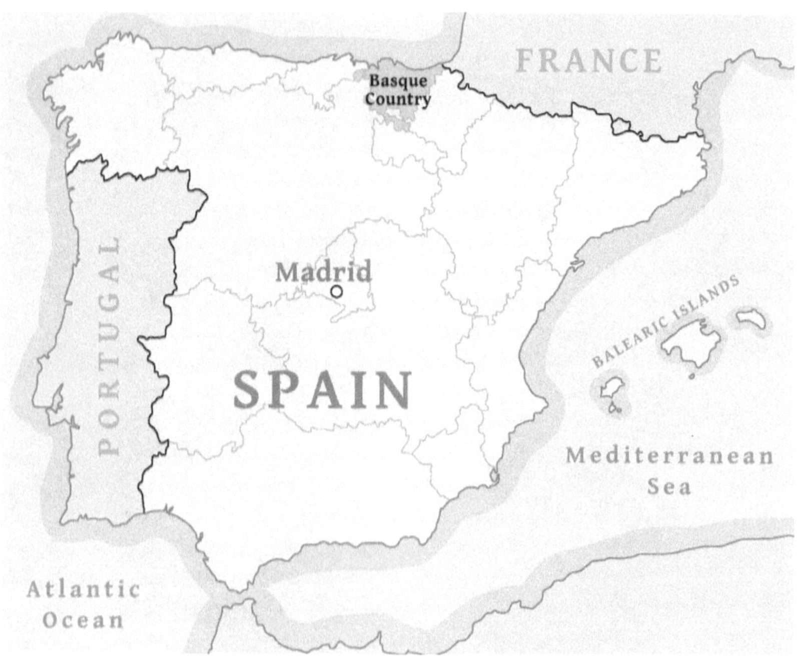

---

[2] "Expelled from Spain," https://www.pbs.org.

Maps of the Americas

"History of Jewish migration—Sephardic and Ashkenazi Jews continued to arrive to the Americas. The first Jewish settlement in Latin America actually took place while royal decrees still banned Jews in Spanish and Portuguese colonies throughout the continent."[3] "There have been Jewish communities in the United States since colonial times…before the American Revolution."[4]

—Central America
—South America
—The Caribbean
—The United States

3   Aviad Moreno, "What Do You Know? Jewish Migration to Latin America (April 8, 2019).
4   "History of the Jews in the United States," Wikipedia.

Foreword

ailing with Columbus is more than the title of this book. *Sailing with Columbus* is a voyage of discovery for the author, Ilean Baltodano. She extends to her readers the invitation to join her in exploring and learning about the arrival of Judaism and Jewish culture in the Americas. She offers the possibility that along the path of this journey, you as the reader may reap, as she has "valuable lessons about strength and courage."

Why does a Gentile—an immigrant to the United States who fled with her family from Nicaragua, someone who describes herself as "not a writer by profession," and someone who labors "with written words in Spanish and English"—undertake a book like this one? "Who will your readers be?" I asked Ilean. She answered, "For those readers who are relatively unacquainted with Jewish people, Jewish culture, and Judaic history, my compact book offers an overview of the complexities of Judaism. Those readers who are familiar with Jewish culture and history may find here a convenient springboard from which to do further research."

This is the invitation: explore what Ilean has written about Jewish history and ethos, search the bibliography, engage with the interviews, travel through time, wonder and marvel at the power of community to sustain life in the depths of adversity and to celebrate life in all seasons.

You are invited.

—Mary Susan Gast, Benicia's poet laureate emerita

Introduction

> Anyone who says writing is
> easy isn't doing it right.
>
> —Amy Joy

Let me introduce myself. I am a naturalized US citizen who was born and raised in Nicaragua. I am not a writer by profession; I labor with written words in Spanish and English. I am not yet a prolific poet, but I am something of a dreamer.

My father, Ricardo Zeledón, has been a profound influence on my writing. He transmitted his emotions through poetry. I was very young, but I still remember when a group of police officers arrested him. The right-wing dictatorship of Anastasio Somoza's government imprisoned him for twelve long months for writing on behalf of the oppressed. Initially, my father was able to escape by running through the house, making his way to the backyard, and jumping over the fence. It is a fact that when you are looking for freedom and safety, you will jump any barrier, any wall, no matter how high it is, whether it is built of wood, cement, steel, or floating border walls with razor wire. For quite some time, he was a fugitive, and later, while conducting a meeting with syndicate union working-class members, he was arrested. His time in prison made him extremely paranoid of individuals in military attire, even afraid of traffic police officers. As a small child, I didn't understand why he was arrested and imprisoned for one long year.

I arrived as a tourist in the United States in 1979 when Jimmy Carter was president. Our family—my husband, our four daughters, and me, pregnant with our fifth child—arrived in California for what we believed would be a three-week vacation. However, the United States soon became our home, and we never moved back to our country.

Nicaragua is described as the land of lakes and volcanoes, poetry, music, boxing, baseball, earthquakes, political instability, dictatorship from left and right, and the land of wealth and poverty. Nicaragua is also known for the poet Ruben Dario, who initiated the Spanish American version of literary modernism. The current Sandinista government is a left-wing dictatorship causing suffering to the population. Many Nicaraguans, including the clergy, women, peasants, students, and businesspeople, have been incarcerated. Nicaragua is a low-income, food-deficit country and one of the poorest in Latin America. I cannot rest easy seeing the Nicaraguan people continue to suffer.

My personal story is candidly shared in both versions (English and Spanish) of my memoir, *Still on Vacation—in the Middle of a Pandemic*, and the Spanish translation, *Todavía de Vacaciones en Medio de la Pandemia.* (These books are widely available, including in public libraries and on Amazon.) Imagine taking a three-week vacation and being afraid to return to your country due to ongoing political unrest. What would you do? For me, as well as for most immigrants, safety is the primary goal. I am reminded of the biblical narrative in the book of Exodus about the enslaved Israelites who finally were able to depart from Egypt in search of the *"land flowing with milk and honey."* As an immigrant, I have always felt a sense of kinship with the Jewish people. Just as the ancient Israelites migrated in search of freedom from oppression and a better life, so too have I. This book pursues my interest in the history of the Jewish people and how they came to the Americas, including the theory that several Jews sailed with Christopher Columbus. Writing on this topic has been both an unbelievable journey and a humbling experience. It is remarkable to me that even when I finished writing about these courageous survivors, I wasn't even close to covering everything.

In May of 1979, I started my fourth year of law school in Nicaragua but only attended classes for two weeks. The political situation in the country worsened and consequently became unsafe. A few weeks prior to our trip, I found an anonymous note that was slipped under our front door. The note read, *"Watch out for your daughters!"* Considering this dire threat, we decided to take a vacation trip to California, expecting to return home as soon as things settled down. Never did it cross our minds that this vacation was going to last a lifetime!

Years passed, and after embarking on my new life in the United States, I completed my education and obtained a bachelor of science degree in organizational behavior and a master of science degree in human resources and organizational development. It was a blessing that I was able to study at a university that made it possible for me to complete my education while working full-time for Chevron and raising my children. Additionally, as it turned out, my husband was diagnosed with cancer, and throughout his illness, I was busy caring for him. Sadly, he eventually passed away.

As an immigrant, I experienced many challenges, including learning English and trying to organize my life around my family. My bachelor's program required me to take three units in religion. I found a course that fit into my schedule, *Heritage: Civilization and the Jews*. At that time, the topic of the Holocaust and Jewish history were not top-of-mind interests for me. Yet as time went by, things shifted. As a curious person by nature, I dream of ventures beyond my normal comfort zone. One day, many years later, I was sorting out the clutter in my library and getting rid of items that fell into the category of donation to goodwill. Under some dusty boxes, I found an interesting research paper I had written in that religion course. This surprise discovery was a pleasant interruption to my cleanup project. With the paper in my hands, I sat down on the floor and began reading the assignment I had written years before.

As I read the wrinkled and yellowed paper, it transported me to historical times of the past as well as to the present of an ancient culture. It is a document filled with information that I gathered while attending college. This paper brought back memories of how hard I had to work since English was my second language. I remember being surrounded by so many fellow students who seemed so smart to me because English was their native language. In my joy and amazement, I decided I would keep this discovery a secret, but I was also going to share it with my friend "Solitude." I am not antisocial, but my friend "Solitude" helps me to understand myself—to reflect and to disconnect from the noise. Having time to myself helps me maintain better relationships by becoming more proactive.

Initially, enrolling in the religion class was just to fulfill the required three units. However, when I found my essay, I felt I wanted to learn more about Jewish culture. Also, I became very interested in the theory that several Jews may have traveled to the New World with Christopher Columbus. In my childhood in Nicaragua, I grew up in close contact with families of Jewish heritage. This included my godmother's family, Elena Arellano de Françeries, whose husband, Raymundo Françeries, was a French Jew, a polite gentleman who had a cute French accent in Spanish.

I believe that things happen for a reason. Organizing my library room reconnected me with something unexpected. Every effect has a cause. When we experience an unexpected event, we might conclude that a benevolent and superior being has caused this episode to happen for a reason. As days went by, this discovery remained in my mind, and along with my friend Solitude, we decided to embark on a new adventure. This adventure has led me to study this subject intensely and to write this book. I knew this task would not be easy, but I was willing to face the challenges that came along the way, including criticism. My developing interest fed my desire to scrutinize, learn, and share this topic with others.

> Take risks. If you win, you will be happy;
> If you lose, you will be wise.
> —Anonymous

Thus, I began this fabulous project that would lead me to explore and learn about Judaism and Jewish culture, not knowing that this adventure was going to teach me valuable lessons about strength and courage. I have learned the importance of perseverance and that following dreams and trusting one's self, regardless of the opinion of others, are indispensable to any endeavor. I invite you to join me on this journey.

Learning about Jewish culture has taught me that life's journey shapes who we are. Challenges and the decisions we make to meet them are a reflection of our inner being. I hope that those who read this story will understand that on Earth, we have to be ready for the trials that come our way. The path of life is full of good and bad. Life is an endless labyrinth with voices that often deceive us and bring us fearful situations. But we must walk with confidence until doubts disappear, facing them with courage, prepared for what awaits us down the road. Climbing any mountain has challenges and requires perseverance and patience to reach the top. Learn from every experience and be humble in acquiring wisdom for the well-being of all. Wisdom is not found in any specific place but rather through continuous study. While I was writing this book, my companion Solitude brought me the serenity that prepared me for the challenges that awaited me on the journey.

As I approach the finish line, I look back and realize that I learned to trust myself and others who willingly supported me. As I researched and wrote, I learned incredible stories about Judaic culture and religion. The next destination was to get this story to my readers. In this new journey, the landscape will be totally different. But in fact, the real treasure is taking the journey, not arriving at the destination.

Am I an expert in this subject? Certainly not. While I was writing, I was learning. Standing at the threshold of a new book is the starting point for a new experience. Why did I decide to write about this topic? Frankly, I was following my instincts, and many times, following my instincts has worked for me. So, dear readers, I hope some of you will be learning. There is always a great deal to learn. As Albert Einstein said, "Once you stop learning, you start dying."

In May 2023, I flew to visit the Netherlands, Belgium, and Germany to visit sites where the Holocaust took place. These places have historically impacted the Jewish population. I have visited museums in these three countries before, but this time, I wanted to immerse myself in the scene of the world's worst-ever crime. I wanted to visit some of these places, such as where Tova Friedman, Anne Frank, and Corrie ten Boom had been. These are locations where the Holocaust took place. Tova Friedman, who was born in Poland, is one of the youngest survivors to have been freed from Auschwitz.

Tova was four years old when she was sent with her parents to a Nazi labor camp. She witnessed atrocities that she could never forget and experienced numerous escapes from death. In January 1945, Tova and her mother hid among corpses. In her book *The Daughter of Auschwitz*, she documents what she saw. Her intention in writing the book was to keep the story of the Holocaust alive at a time when it was in danger of fading from memory. Anne Frank wrote her diary, which became her companion while in hiding in the secret annex of a building in Amsterdam, Holland. In another province of the Netherlands, the city of Haarlem was where Corrie ten Boom was born. She was a Christian woman who risked her life hiding Jews during the Nazi occupation by active participation in the Dutch underground. Before the trip, I refreshed my knowledge of French, but most of the time, I didn't need it. I'm glad English and Spanish are such universal languages.

During World War II, Adolf Hitler and the Nazi Party took control of Germany, transforming it into a dictatorship. In 1940, Germany, despite Dutch neutrality, invaded and occupied the Netherlands. Nazi Germany also conquered Belgium in May 1940. This was the second time in less than thirty years that Germany had occupied Belgium. Hitler and Nazi Germany brought persecution, deportation, and mass murder to the Jews (as well as to individuals among the Roma, political undesirables, the disabled, etc.).

In this book, I will be discussing people with many years of genealogy and with an incredible tradition. Additionally, I am sharing the theory that Christopher Columbus brought Jewish individuals to the New World. I am writing with admiration and respect. I am putting together an overview of a culture that has always shown courage, determination, perseverance, integrity, excellence, and faith in one God.

I did a good deal of research, although it never seemed enough. I have asked the Creator of the universe for direction because I want to be objective while unveiling information about this culture. This is a theme about a nation that believes in the holy "I am who I am." In my life, I have taken many risks, and I feel that I am taking a big one in writing this book. What I am going to share with you is based on research, as listed in the bibliography, as well as on interviews with laypersons and rabbis. When I announced to others that I was going to write about the Jewish people, I received some criticism. In fact, I began to question what I was doing. After all, this topic is broad and is not in my personal area of expertise. However, I was determined to persevere because I felt a desire to share my modicum of knowledge in order to convey what I had learned about Jewish culture.

Always listen to your heart.
It may be on your left, but it's always right.
—Anonymous

The experience of researching the many aspects of Jewish culture and putting together this book has been an incredibly gratifying learning curve and a humbling experience. This process opened doors of continued discovery for me, and I hope it will do so for my readers as well. Whenever I paused researching or writing, I felt empty because my goal was to make my book a reality. The amount of hardships that the Jewish people have gone through since Jacob, the Hebrew patriarch, who was the grandson of Abraham, the son of Isaac and Rebekah, and the ancestor of the people of Israel, is hard to believe. In fact, God changed Jacob's name to "Israel." This is a story of enslavement, migration, and a continual struggle for freedom and survival. The noteworthy fact about my personal journey of becoming acquainted with Jewish culture is that my troubles and anxieties diminished while writing because the story and sufferings of the Jewish people are one of a kind.

Prior to writing this book, I experienced how hard it is to be an immigrant seeking freedom and safety. Writing this book has opened my eyes and helped me realize how fortunate I am. Despite all the changes I have experienced as an immigrant—adapting to a new country, losing through confiscation the home I left, adding a new language to my daily life, and adapting to a new culture—I learned to apply grim persistence to overcome challenges. By always remembering where I came from, how can I forget how blessed I am? I know I am not the first immigrant to have to cross borders, rivers, and oceans. Some have died trying. Putting all these factors and more into the equation pales in comparison to what the Jewish people have gone through and continue to experience. And I am inspired by their tenacity, faith, and resilience.

Many times, I asked myself whether I should continue writing this book, but the support I have received from friends, local writers, and the Benicia Public Library has inspired me to carry on in pursuit of my goal. The topic of my book is compelling. Although sharing my personal bilingual style is somewhat scary for me, I have learned not to shy away from criticism. There is the belief that when you write, you become a writer. It is so liberating to share ideas and research with strangers. I kept on writing from my heart without hesitating. My advice is that you should do the same. There is a potential book in every one of us.

Ilean Baltodano

Chapter 1

The Resilient Nation

Since the beginning of human history, people have been longing and searching for assurance that life has a purpose and that death is not the end. People have worshipped many gods according to the patterns of each culture. Some cultures worshipped the sun and nature. For example, the ancient Egyptians deified the Nile River with the god Hapi. One of the most important gods was Osiris, the god of death, who also ruled over the regular flooding of the Nile.[5] Other gods and goddesses represented animals as possessing incredible power and having the ability to transmit wisdom, strength, and fertility. The pharaohs, too, were regarded as divinities. The ancient Egyptians built pyramids of incredible beauty, and how they accomplished these amazing feats of architectural engineering is still a mystery to us today.

There are many theories about God and how the world was created. For the Jewish people, before the practice of archaeology, the main source of information about the ancient world was the Old Testament of the Bible—a book that is universally known. The *Torah* is the compilation of the first five books of the Hebrew Bible, namely the books of Genesis, Exodus, Leviticus, Numbers, and Deuteronomy. In these first five books of the Bible is traced the genealogy of the Jews. This genealogy includes a line of God-fearing men—Abraham, Isaac, Jacob, and Joseph. Yet even before these righteous men appear, the *Torah* speaks of Eden, a garden surrounded by water from the rivers Tigris and Euphrates. These two great rivers that define the area of Mesopotamia

---

[5] Encyclopedia Britannica Online.

flow south from the mountains of the Armenian Highlands through the Syrian and Arabian Deserts and empty into the Persian Gulf. Ancient Mesopotamia relied upon these rivers to provide drinking water, agricultural irrigation, and major transportation routes.

It is significant that in Genesis 1, the *Torah* tells of God's creation of the world and its creatures. The first human being is called "Adam." The name derives from the Hebrew word for "earth"—the red clay is called "adama." All this began in Mesopotamia, the part of the Middle East now known as modern Iraq. More specifically, the area encompassed present-day Iraq and Kuwait and also parts of Iran, Syria, and Turkey. This is the setting where the biblical narrative of the dramatic history of the Jewish people begins.

To broaden my understanding of how Judaism and Jewish culture have evolved from ancient times until today, I embarked on an odyssey to learn more. I had many questions about Judaic culture, such as, "Who are the Jews?" "Where did they come from?" "Why did they flee Egypt?" After reading many books, visiting several places where the Holocaust took place, and interviewing people, I felt inspired and better equipped to process what I learned by writing this book. And I enhanced my knowledge of the history of the Holocaust, what brought about the creation of the State of Israel, and what is the status and location of the Jewish community around the world, especially the Jewish community in the Americas.

I also had simpler questions, such as—"What is a typical Jewish meal?" I found some answers in the book *A Field Guide to the Jewish People*, in which the authors Dave Barry, Adam Mansbach, and Alan Zweibel use comic stories to make readers laugh while beginning to develop an appreciation of the inner workings of Judaism.

So let me begin with my first question—"Who are the Jews?" The Jewish people can be described as an ethnoreligious group. Ethnoreligious groups are communities united by a common faith, which, through intermarriage, developed cultural and ancestral ties.[6] The Jewish people are not only a race and not only a religion. There is a strong argument, supported by Jewish and non-Jewish cultural theorists, that Jews are not

---

[6] Ethnoreligious group, https://en.m.wikipedia.org

a race. Jews historically have defined themselves as a people—the descendants of Abraham, Isaac, and Jacob.[7] They also describe themselves as a tribe unified by a common religious and ethnic background. There are currently, as of September 2023, about 15.7 million Jews around the world, representing 0.2 percent of the global population. Some live in Israel, some live in the United States, and others are scattered in various nations throughout the world—all with a common heritage.

This Judaic heritage has carried a tradition that includes a tangible and intangible culture. The shared bond of belonging to a community has resulted in creating a Judaic cultural identity that has evolved through the centuries of ancient and modern history. Those who identify as Jews today are heirs to a long-inherited tradition and culture that has been passed down from previous generations. Against the backdrop of history, the Jewish people have developed resilience and have demonstrated the determination to survive against all odds.

Who were the ancient Israelites?[8] Over the course of many years, these people who were first identified as Canaanites eventually became known as Hebrews, Israelites, and finally, the Jews. The word "Israel" comes from Abraham's grandson, Jacob, who was renamed "Israel." The Israelites are the people whom the Hebrew Bible describes as the direct descendants of any of the sons of the patriarch Jacob—later called "Israel." In Genesis 32:22–32, Jacob is sleeping and finds himself wrestling with someone:

> A man came and fought with Jacob until just before daybreak. They kept on wrestling until the man said, "Let go of me! It's almost daylight." "You can't go until you bless me," Jacob replied. Then the man asked, "What is your name?" "Jacob," he answered. The man said, "From now on, your name will no longer be Jacob. You will be called Israel because you have wrestled with God and with men, and you have won." (Genesis 32:22–32)

---

[7]   The Book of Genesis.
[8]   Israelite Tribe.

According to the biblical narrative, the site was named Peniel, "Face of God" by Jacob. "It is because I saw God face to face, and yet my life was spared" (Genesis 32:30). His descendants are also collectively called Israelites, including converts.

Currently, there are several different branches of observance. The main branches include Orthodox, Conservative, Reform, Reconstructionist, and Humanist. Orthodox Judaism is the most traditional form of modern Judaism, and Orthodox Jews comprise the most theologically conservative branch of Judaism. Although Messianic Jews claim to maintain their Jewish identity while acknowledging Jesus as the Messiah, "Messianic Judaism is a modernist and syncretic movement of Protestant Christianity that incorporates some elements of Judaism and other Jewish traditions into evangelicalism."[9] Jews, unlike Christians, do not acknowledge Jesus as the Messiah promised to Israel. They regard the Torah, written and oral, as revealed by God to Moses on Mount Sinai and faithfully transmitted ever since. With the Covenant, the God of Moses promised his blessings to his people. He said, "I am the Lord your God, who brought you out of Egypt, out of the land of slavery" (Exodus 20:2). God gave to Moses a set of ten laws that the Israelites should follow, the Ten Commandments, which became the covenant God made with all Jewish people at Mount Sinai.

The resilient Jewish people have a fascinating cultural history. Jews have made significant contributions to every area of human endeavor, including literature, philosophy, music, nutrition, medicine, biology, chemistry, physics, etc. Some excellent poetry is found in the book of Psalms and the Song of Solomon:

> To everything there is a season,
> And a time to every purpose under the heaven:
> A time to be born and a time to die;
> A time to plant, and a time to reap.
> —Ecclesiastes 3

---

[9] Messianic Judaism, https://en.m.wikipedia.org.

In the numerous spiritual narratives found in the Bible, there are many meaningful scriptures of timeless value for the generations.

The legacy of Judaic heritage received a glowing compliment from the second United States president, John Adams, in the following excerpt from a letter he wrote:

> I will insist the Hebrews have [contributed] more to civilize men than any other nation. If I was an atheist and believed in blind eternal fate, I should still believe that fate had ordained the Jews to be the most essential instrument for civilizing the nations...they are the most glorious nation that ever inhabited this Earth. The Romans and their empire were but a bubble in comparison to the Jews. They have given religion to three-quarters of the globe and have influenced the affairs of mankind more and more happily than any other nation, ancient or modern.
>
> John Adams
> Letter to François Adrian van der Kemp
> (February 16, 1808)
> Pennsylvania Historical Society

Chapter 2

Jewish Values and Culture

Jewish culture respects tradition, family, and work. The most meaningful parts of Jewish life occur at home rather than in public. It is said that families are the building blocks of society. Jewish law and tradition highlight the centrality of the family and home. Judaism recognizes that each parent has something special to give to their children to contribute to their religious, educational, emotional, social, and material needs.

We are all prone to embrace the values by which we were raised. These are values such as honesty, integrity, kindness, courage, and respect for elders and family. Most individuals tend to observe the values of their society because they were raised within that particular culture. There are some theories about how values might differ among groups within a culture. Culture, on the other hand, can be defined as *all the ways of life, including arts, beliefs, and institutions of a population that are passed down from generation to generation, such as principles, traditions, and rituals.*[10]

Throughout recorded history, since the biblical Abraham and Sarah, the Jewish people have been on the move. According to the book of Genesis, Abraham left Ur in Mesopotamia because *God called him to found a new nation in an undesignated land that he later learned was Canaan.* Later, in the book of Exodus, to escape Pharaoh's death penalty, Moses led the Israelites out of Egypt, and they wandered in the desert for forty years before finally arriving in the promised land

---

[10] "Culture," https://sphweb.bumc.bu.edu.

of Canaan. Since the diaspora and continually up to the modern era, and even up to this day, the forces of anti-Semitic violence and restrictions imposed upon Jewish inhabitants have forced Jews to flee to safer places. Consequently, the daily life of Jews has evolved in relation to wherever they resettled, and Judaic culture had to adapt to the new local customs and laws. Therefore, the passage of time has caused a significant impact on Jewish culture.

However, despite all the pogroms, ghettos, legal restrictions on owning land and property and on limiting education and professions—and perhaps even partly because of all forms of anti-Semitism, Jews clung to their religious beliefs and practices, thereby maintaining their sense of identity. And embracing their identity enabled the survival of the Jewish people and Judaic culture. The Jewish people have passed down their customs and beliefs. Over time, different branches of Judaism have evolved.

In ancient times, for the two centuries up to the year 70 CE, when the Romans destroyed the second temple, there were four Jewish sects: Pharisees, Sadducees, Essenes, and Zealots.

The Pharisees were members of a group that believed in the resurrection of the dead via the afterlife and in following legal traditions that were ascribed not only to the Bible but also to the Oral Law, "the traditions of the fathers." They were usually the common people dedicated to following and interpreting both the Oral Law and the Written Law as found in the Torah. What is most significant about the Pharisees is that their beliefs survived and resulted in the rabbinic tradition that has evolved into what we know as modern Judaism.[11]

The Sadducees were the religious sect of the financial and social elite of Jerusalem. They were the aristocrats and the wealthy merchants who took pride in their status and wealth. They did not believe in the resurrection of the dead, whereas the Pharisees did. Sadducees rejected the notion of spirits or angels. They didn't believe that an afterlife and resurrection of the dead were in line with the Written Law of the Torah.[12]

---

[11] Matthew 23:2–7 and Mark 7:8–9.
[12] Luke 3:2

The Essenes[13] were a sect or school of philosophy with two branches: some were celibate, some disdained marriage, and some adopted children. The others believed that marriage and procreation were needed if the group was to continue and not disappear. Their community was hierarchical, structured, and disciplined. Disliking the mainstream lifestyle of Jerusalem, they retreated from the city and set up an alternative way of life in the desert. However, there is no evidence that their sect survived after the Temple was destroyed.

The Zealots[14] were an aggressive political party whose concern for the national and religious life of the Jewish people led them to despise even Jews who sought peace and conciliation with the Roman authorities. Their passion for freedom and strong faith in God caused a group of Zealots to establish a hideout from the Romans in the desert atop Mount Masada, overlooking the Dead Sea. According to the Zealot traitor/Roman historian Josephus, the entire community of at least 960 people committed mass suicide so as not to become conquered and enslaved by the Romans.

At the start of the modern period—beginning around 1750, the religious division continued to increase notably, but still this population was still regarded by others as Jews. Throughout the seventeenth and eighteenth centuries, different groups began to give emphasis to diverse foundations of their faith, including ceremonial and spiritual practices. These include four separate variants of Judaism: *Haredim*, *Dati*, *Masorti*, and *Hiloni*. This designation applies to Jews outside the US, including Israel.

Haredi is a subcategory of Orthodox Judaism, also referred to as ultrareligious or ultraorthodox. The Haredim merely follows God's law as it was originally prescribed. The term *Haredi* comes from the Hebrew word meaning "tremble." Thus, *Haredi* connotes having immense respect for God and his law above all else.

Dati literally means religious and can be translated as "modern Orthodox." The Datim are traditionally observant—for example, keeping kosher (following the dietary laws) and observing the

---

[13] "Essenes in Judean Society," https://blog.cup.com.

[14] "Zealots/Essenes, Jewish Sects," https://www.britannica.com

Sabbath.[15] The Sabbath is a day of religious observance and abstinence from work from Friday evening to Saturday evening. The Romans ridiculed the Jews about the Sabbath, but we have none but the Jews to thank for our weekend. Christians adapted the Jewish Shabbat to Sunday in the second and third centuries.

The *Masorti* category of Jews is the most diverse of the Jewish groups. They encompass a large middle ground between the Orthodox groups and secular Jews. Some Masorti Jews say that religion is somewhat important in their lives—as opposed to very important or not too/not at all important. Their status corresponds to what in the US is known as Conservative Judaism.

The *Hilonim* are secular Jews. This is a social category in Israel designating the least religious segment among the Jewish public. In 2018, according to the *Israel Central Bureau of Statistics* survey, 43.2 percent of Jews were identified as *Hilonim*.

The term *Zionism* is a movement whose name is derived from the word Zion. Zion[16] is a hill in the city of Jerusalem, one of the city's seven hills. The Zionist movement, created by Theodor Herzl in the 1890s, envisioned a permanent homeland for the Jewish people. The creation of Israel in 1948 was the fulfillment of this dream of an independent Jewish state.

At the present time, Jews live all around the globe. However, the majority of Jews live in either of two countries; the United States and Israel have the largest Jewish populations worldwide—six million in the US and almost seven million in Israel. While Jews comprise a minority in the US, in Israel, almost 80 percent of the population is Jewish. After World War II ended, members of the Zionist movement focused on completing the establishment of a permanent homeland for Holocaust survivors, an independent Jewish state.

The years since the founding of the State of Israel in 1948 have been characterized by conflict with the neighboring Arab states as well as with the Arab Palestinians within Israel. The Palestinian peo-

---

[15] "Sabbath to Sunday," https://en.m.wikipedia.org>wiki.

[16] "Zionism/Definition, History, Examples, and Facts," https://www.britytanica.com.

ple, also referred to as Palestinian Arabs, are an ethno-national group who have inhabited the region of Palestine over the millennia and who are today culturally and linguistically Arabs. The United Nations approved a plan to partition Palestine into a Jewish and Arab state in 1947, but the Arabs rejected the plan. In May 1948, Israel was officially declared an independent state. As the only democracy in the entire Middle East, Israel is a great partner to the United States. The bond between these two countries is very strong.

Zionism – a movement for (originally) the reestablishment and (now) the development and protection of a Jewish nation in what is currently Israel. It was established as a political organization in 1897 under Theodor Herzl, who declared the following:

> If you will, it is no dream…it is true that
> we aspire to our ancient land. But what we want
> in that ancient land is a new blossoming of the
> Jewish spirit.

Chaim Azriel Weizmann served as president of the Zionist Organization from 1921 to 1931 and again from 1935 to 1946 and subsequently became the first president of Israel in 1949. Dr. Weizmann said the following:

> "Independence is never given to a people,
> it has to be earned; and once earned, must be
> defended."[17]

The *Knesset* (Hebrew for "Assembly"), the Israeli parliament, first convened on February 14, 1949, following the January 20 elections. The main function of the Knesset is to enact laws. The Knesset is both the legislative body and the house of representatives of Israel.

---

[17] "Israel's 70th birthday," Weizmann Institute of Science, https://www.weizmann.ac.il>sections.

It is a fact that in Israel, Jews are united by homeland but divided into very different groups.

The Jewish culture is incredibly vast, diverse, and complex. Any study of Jewish culture might investigate aspects of religion, race, moral philosophy, technology, legal systems, and a variety of historical and local customs—not to mention literature, art, music, dance, cuisine, attire, family relations, gender, and many more topics. It's no secret that Israeli inventions have changed the world. To truly understand how Jewish culture has evolved into its dynamic current state of development, it is important to look at the Judaic past.

The origin of Judaic culture goes back to the twelve tribes of Israel. God changed Jacob's name to Israel, meaning: *let God prevail.*[18]

In the Hebrew culture, the name of God is important, and the many names of God help us understand more of his power. And, as Psalm 9 mentions, knowing God's name helps one to trust Him.

These are the Hebrew names for God:
–YHWH–
"To be"
–Adonai–
"My Lord"
–Elohim–
"God" or "Deity"
–Shaddai–
"The Almighty"
–Tzevaot–
"The God of the armies of Israel"
–Ehyeh Asher Ehyeh–
"I am who I am"

As mentioned before, in the aspect of religion, their G-d is too holy to write. They omit the vowels, as in *"JHWH"* for Jehovah.[19]

---

[18] Genesis 35:9–10
[19] Exodus 6:3 and Psalm 83:18

The Hebrew calendar is richly crammed with holidays and observances that honor religious and cultural traditions.[20] One example of a tradition is the practice of placing a mezuzah on the doorframe to the right of the front door. The mezuzah is a decorative case that contains a piece of parchment that is inscribed with a specific prayer from Deuteronomy 6:4–9 and 11:13–21. Some of the most notable holidays include Passover, Rosh Hashanah, and Yom Kippur.

At Passover, Jewish families retell the story of the exodus from Egypt with the help of a booklet called the Haggadah that contains the narrative, blessings, prayers, and songs. The event is called a Seder (which is a Hebrew word meaning "order" and involves a celebratory meal that begins with snacking on ritual foods that represent aspects of the Biblical exodus story). Matzoh is a cracker that represents the unleavened bread of the ancient Israelites. Salt water and bitter herbs represent the tears and unhappiness of the Hebrew slaves to Pharaoh. The ten plagues are listed and named. And charoset, the walnut and apple dish moistened with wine, represents the mortar for the bricks that the children of Israel were forced to build with for cruel Pharaoh's pyramid construction project. A central part of the ritual meal is when the youngest child in the family recites the "Four Questions." The participants then read the liturgy that gives the answers. Another special ritual feature is pouring a glass of wine on the table for the wished-for Messiah, the prophet Elijah, and then later at the appointed time in the Seder, opening the door to allow him to enter the home.

Rosh Hashanah is a very important Jewish holiday. This is the traditional Jewish New Year. Together, Rosh Hashanah and Yom Kippur are known as the High Holidays. Yom Kippur is the holiest day of the Jewish year and marks a time for atonement through fasting and prayer. Hanukkah is also known as the Festival of Lights. This holiday commemorates the restoration of the Temple in Jerusalem, where, according to tradition, Jews rose up against their Greek-Syrian oppressors in the Maccabean Revolt (167–160 BCE). Most observant Jews attend synagogue services on Rosh Hashanah and Yom Kippur.

---

[20] "Jewish Exodus 6:3 and Psalm 83:18 Holidays," https://en.m.wikipedia.org.

In Judaic culture, music and dance have played a central role in the expression of joy and emotions. These social activities can be found incorporated into religious observance among virtually most Jewish denominations. Synagogue congregations usually have a cantor (*chazan*) to assist the rabbi as a prayer leader who sings liturgical music.

Many Jewish family rituals represent transitions from one state in life to another: birth, adulthood, marriage, and death. Carefully chosen names are considered significant in the Jewish tradition. There is a belief that the name given to an infant will determine the child's character. For example, *David* means *beloved*. The name *Sarah* means *princess*. Names can be derived from the birth order—such as firstborn or the name of a child who has come to take the place of a child who has died in childhood. Nowadays, American Jewish babies are often given a Hebrew name in addition to their English name.

Have you ever had your name changed? An interesting fact about names is found in the Bible. The act of their receiving new names represented them becoming something new. This happened to Abram and Sarai: No longer shall your name be Abram, but your name shall be Abraham…as for Sarai, your wife, you shall not call her Sarai, but Sarah shall be her name. Because Jacob was faithful, the Lord gave him the special name of "Israel," which means "one who prevails with God."[21] Jesus gave Simon the name *Cephas*,[22] meaning "stone," which is translated as "Petros" in Greek, becoming "Peter" in English. In the modern world, when monarchs ascend to the throne, they often take on new royal names to signify their new status.

Although in the United States, circumcision is a standard medical procedure for male newborns, with observant Jewish families, circumcision is predominantly performed as a religious ritual called a *brit milah* or *bris*. Traditional Jewish law specifies that *all baby boys be circumcised on the eighth day of life*. The circumcision is the physical representation of the covenant between God and Abraham described in the Old Testament.[23] Early Christianity did not encourage circumcision because

---

[21] Genesis 17.

[22] John 1:42.

[23] Genesis 17:10–14

the apostle Paul believed faith was more important. Muslims also practice circumcision as a confirmation of their relationship with God.

Cuisine and faith are important elements of Jewish culture. Special dishes that relate to the specific theme the holiday observes are eaten on different holidays. The Jewish culture has dietary laws that are followed strictly by Orthodox households and at least partially by observant families. *Kashruth* is the system of dietary laws that dictate what foods are kosher.[24] In Hebrew, *kosher* means fit or proper. Food that is kosher is fit for consumption by Jewish people. A primary tenet of keeping kosher is to separate meat and dairy ingredients so that these two are never combined as ingredients and do not occur together in a particular meal. This directive extends to tableware and cooking tools. Therefore, a kosher kitchen has double sets of pots and pans, dishes, etc.—one set for meat and another for dairy.

Certain foods, notably pork and shellfish, are forbidden. Vegetables, fruits, fish, eggs, and other foods that are neither dairy nor meat are known as *pareve*. Generally, Orthodox and ultraorthodox Jewish families keep kosher. Observing the *dietary laws of kashrut* is a way for strictly observant Jews to show reverence to God and feel connected to their heritage. This is a tradition that has eroded in recent generations, as individuals have opted to live a less observant lifestyle than their parents. However, some of these more assimilated Jewish families often continue to practice some aspects of kashruth to a lesser degree, thereby continuing to respect their heritage.

Diet is intrinsic to Jewish ritual, life, and culture. It appears that there is no way anyone can practice Judaism religiously or culturally without enjoying good nutrition. According to Lori Stein and Ronald H. Isaacs, authors of the engaging book *Jewish Food and Faith,* Jewish food is wonderfully simmered in a rich broth of history, culture, geography, and religion. The relation between diet, ethical values, and tradition is a pillar of Jewish culture. The book *Let's Eat: Jewish Food and Faith* quips that the story of Judaism can be condensed into nine words: "*They tried to kill us. We survived. Let's eat.*"

---

[24] Leviticus 11.

Jewish gastronomy extends to a wide range of international fare. Bagels originated in the Jewish communities of Poland. Latkes are potato pancakes that are a staple of Hanukkah celebrations. Matzo ball soup and Ashkenazi chicken soup with dumplings made from matzo meal are Passover Seder essentials that are enjoyed year-round as well. Moreover, chicken soup has been dubbed "Jewish penicillin" and is the absolute best when you've got the flu. Kugel is a noodle delectable casserole. Braiding a challah loaf for Shabbat is fun. As Jewish people have migrated around the globe, different regions have developed their own unique dishes.

The bar mitzvah for thirteen-year-old Jewish boys is a time-honored tradition that has evolved to also allow girls to become bat mitzvah at twelve or thirteen. This culmination of Torah and Hebrew study is a rite of passage that recognizes the youth as a responsible member of the congregation. Needless to say, this is a big deal, a graduation of sorts that is often accompanied by an elaborate party celebration after the temple ceremony is concluded.

Attire is an essential feature of Jewish culture. For example, the skull cap known as a *kippah* or *yarmulke is* traditionally worn at all times by Orthodox Jewish men to demonstrate reverence for God. Jewish men wear kippahs to Shabbat and holiday services in the synagogue and also at religious events outside the temple and/or in the home. Prayer shawls are worn to services by observant Jewish men and are also an important adornment for the bar or bat mitzvah student's ceremony.

Hebrew literature has continually evolved throughout the ages. The Old Testament of the Hebrew Bible is the most important work of ancient Hebrew literature. Judaic culture possesses an ancient and large classical literature. The Talmud is the central text of Rabbinic Judaism and the primary source of Jewish religious law and Jewish theology. The Midrashim is a mode of biblical interpretation. Together, these foundational collections of books hold essential religious and cultural influence.

The Bible is a work of monumental artistry. As a literature of faith, the Old Testament is a collection of religious scriptures that are sacred not only to Judaism and Christianity but also to Samaritanism,

Islam, and many other religions. It can be broken into various classifications of literature. The Bible is made up of many books using diverse types of literature. Some of the authors have used unique literary forms. In some instances, they present ideas in prose or story format, while in others, a prayer or song in a poetic form. While reading the Bible, the reader will encounter letters, laws, rules, history, prayer, parables, and an incredible genealogy. Many readers personally enjoy and never get tired of reading the Bible. Its content is amazing, and the text contains beautiful language, even though it took over 1,600 years and forty God-inspired men to compose it. "All Scripture is God-breathed and is useful for teaching, rebuking, correcting, and training in righteousness, so that the servant of God may be thoroughly equipped for every good work."[25]

> Kavod: Hebrew for honor and respect
> Treat others with respect; follow the Golden Rule
> Be tolerant of differences
> Use good manners, not bad language
> Be considerate of the feelings of others
> Don't threaten, hit or hurt anyone
> Deal peacefully with anger, insults and disagreements
> Honor your father and mother
> that you may long endure on the land that
> Adonai your God has assigned to you. (Exodus 20:12)

Kavod is also used as a title to address judges, the president, or the prime minister of Israel. It is a title meaning "Your Honor" or "Your Excellency."

"The heavens declare the Kavod of God."

---

[25] Timothy 3:16–17

Chapter 3

The Diaspora

So, Daniel was brought before the king, and
the king said to him, are you Daniel, one of the
exiles my father the king brought from Judah?
—Daniel 5:13

This ancient Greek word *diaspora* means dispersion or scattering. It describes people who have left their home country, usually involuntarily, to go to foreign countries. Much of Jewish history is a story of migrations due to fleeing persecution. The dispersion of Israelites out of their ancient ancestral homeland, along with their religious traditions, practices, and beliefs, from the land of Israel led to their subsequent settlement in other parts of the globe. The growth of diaspora Jewish communities has been a gradual process that has occurred over the centuries as a consequence of the Assyrian destruction of Israel, the Babylonian destruction of Judah, Persian and Greek domination, the Roman conquest, and the subsequent rule of Christians and Muslims.

The Bible mentions the diaspora of Jews exiled from Israel by the Babylonians.[26] The king of Judah, for three years, refused to pay taxes to Babylon. As a result, the Babylonians declared war on Judah and captured Jerusalem. The Jewish people were forcefully removed from their homeland and taken to Babylon. The Babylonian captivity was a severe tragedy for the Jews and their culture when they

---

[26] Jeremiah 29.

became enslaved in a foreign land. Needing to make the best out of this cruel situation resulted in considerable adaptation. First, the Jews leveraged whatever valuable skills they possessed and were put to work; this trend allowed educated Jews to advance their social status. Second, they learned and assimilated much of the Babylonian culture and history. Later, when Cyrus the Great of Persia released them, some of the Jews became skilled merchants. For those who returned home, a new temple was built in Jerusalem. From this time onward, the Jews began to create a literary and cultural history that developed into the foundation of Judaism.

There was a dispersion of Jews in the Greek and Roman world from the third century BC onward. As a consequence, large communities of Jews developed in Egypt, Antioch in Syria, Turkey, and Asia Minor, as well as in Greece, the Italian peninsula, especially around Rome, the South of France, and even Spain. By the end of the first century BC, a Greek geographer named Strabo observed that you cannot go anywhere in the civilized world without meeting a Jew. It is important to note that Christianity also spread in those areas. During this time, the apostle Paul began his missionary journeys, and some Jews converted to Christianity. Paul used synagogues to teach the Scriptures to the Jewish community. As you can see, the history of the diaspora, the evolution of synagogues, the Torah and holy scriptures, and the progress of Christianity are all interconnected.

Due to increased migration during the Middle Ages, the Jews of Europe and the Mediterranean communities became associated into two groups, according to geographical location. *Ashkenazim* are Jews who can trace their ancestry back to areas of Central and Eastern Europe. Ashkenazim traditionally have spoken Yiddish, the Jewish lingua franca, among themselves. Yiddish derives from medieval German, with the addition of words from Hebrew and several modern languages. Today, Yiddish is spoken mainly in the United States, Israel, and Russia. Over eighty percent of Jewish people today are *Ashkenazim.*[27] The rest of worldwide Jewry are *Sephardim,*[28] Jews

---

[27] Ashkenaz: Meaning: Germany.
[28] www.jewfaq.org.

of Spanish or Portuguese descent, with their own distinctive set of customs, rituals, and cuisine. Ladino is a language offshoot from Spanish, spoken by some Sephardi Jews whose ancestors likely fled the Spanish Inquisition of 1492. In Israel, the Jewish population is split into nearly equal numbers of Ashkenazim and Sephardim. Many of the Sephardim living there today had to leave Arab countries when or subsequent to when Israel achieved statehood in 1948.[29] Therefore, many Sephardi individuals are also fluent in Arabic. A prime example of the nomadic journey of the Jewish population via the diaspora or Jewish exile can be found in the biblical story of the exodus from Egypt. Therefore, the annual retelling of the first exodus during the celebration of Passover has a special resonance for most Jews, especially those who are acquainted with their ethnic and familial history.

The divine guidance of the original exodus story is poetic and, therefore, lends a healing ray of compassion to the subsequent flights of Jews from wherever they resided.

> By day, the Lord went ahead of them in a
> pillar of cloud to guide them on their way and
> by night in a pillar of fire to give them light, so,
> they could travel by day or night. (Exodus 13:21)

Since the end of the nineteenth century, most Jewish immigrants have ended up in cities, where they became prime movers in the industrialization of their adoptive homelands. In the 1940s, Jews comprised 3.7 percent of the national population.[30]

---

[29] "Creation of Israel, 1948—Milestones: 1945–1952—Office of the Historian," https://history.state.gov>milestones.

[30] "History of the Jews in the United States," https://en.m.wikipedia.org/wiki/Am.

Heroic Jews

Your story of endurance is incredible.
You have survived much suffering
Including the genocidal enemies who murdered
millions.
You watered with your blood
the soil of a nation that will never die.
You are scattered all over the globe,
yet you represent only one nation.

—Ilean Baltodano

Chapter 4

The Chosen People

Scripture reveals a prevailing belief that Jews are God's chosen people. The idea of the Israelites being chosen by God is found in the book of Deuteronomy, which reviews for the Israelites some of their history. Starting with their flight from enslavement in Egypt, the narrative describes their reaching Mount Horeb, where Moses received the Ten Commandments of the law, transferred authority to Joshua, and died. Deuteronomy means "Second Law." The previous generation—the rebellious people who were present when the law was given at Mount Sinai—had already died. Therefore, it was necessary to repeat the law for the benefit of the new generation. The instructions contained in Deuteronomy are specifically addressed to this new generation.

When in Deuteronomy Moses reviews the recent history of the Israelites during the past forty years, he reminds them that God selected them not because of their numbers or power—in fact, they were and always have been a fraction of the human population—but upon the condition of their acceptance of their covenant with the Lord. The central message of this book instructs the Israelites that if they love and serve the Lord, they will be blessed in the promised land. They are chosen to be a light unto the nations and to exemplify the covenant with God as described in the Torah, the first five books of the Old Testament. Nevertheless, there is also a strong affirmation that God has a relationship with all humankind. In fact, Moses refers to the "God of the spirits of all flesh."[31] According to the Bible, "humanity" originated through one man, Adam, in demonstration of God's greatness.

There are conservative Judaism views about the theory of the chosen people. According to the Israel Democracy Institute, approximately two-thirds of Israeli Jews believe that Jews are the chosen. Those who believe in this concept that Jews are the chosen accept the obligation to be a light unto the nations and to exemplify the covenant with God as described in the Torah. This interpretation, however, does not preclude a belief that God has a relationship with all humankind. In an entry in *The Jewish Encyclopedia* of a hundred years ago, the following assessment appears:

> Israel is of all nations the most willful or headstrong one, and the Torah was to give it the right scope and power of resistance, or else the world could not have withstood its fierceness.

> The Nation of Israel is likened to the olive. Just as this fruit yields its precious oil only after being much pressed and squeezed, so Israel's destiny is one of great oppression and hardship, in order that it may thereby give forth its illuminating wisdom. Poverty is the quality most befitting Israel as the chosen people. Only on account of its good works is Israel among the nations "as the lily among thorns," or "as wheat among the chaff."[32]

The Chosen happens to be the title of a novel by Chaim Potok that was first published in 1967. Although a work of fiction, the book presents real themes about how Jewish culture was evolving in the United States during the 1940s. The narrative describes the

---

[31] Jeremiah 32:27.

[32] From the Jewish Encyclopedia, originally published between 1901–1906.

Jewish community of New York City as divided into two camps—one group pulling toward modernism and the other toward retaining all traditional values.

Currently and for many centuries, Jews are scattered all over the world because of their constant relocation for safety and freedom. It is likely that this situation has impacted traditional Judaic perspectives—some moving toward secularism, others toward modernism, and those who have retained many of the traditional values. Such a struggle between traditional and modern values can readily be observed among other faiths worldwide, including denominations within Christianity.

We no longer speak of Israelites outside of the Bible. *Israeli* refers to persons who were born in the modern State of Israel or, in general, those who live there, regardless of their origin, language, or religion. *Hebrew* refers to language and literature—whether biblical or liturgical or the revived modern Hebrew language. For school children in Israel, the ancient text of the Bible is very accessible, as the ancient language is markedly close to the everyday modern Hebrew language.

The Chosen

It is late at night.
I am dreaming while I am awake.
My dream is a desire for a better world.
I am playing the keyboard
not of my piano, but my laptop
waiting for my brain and my heart
to tell my fingers how to start.

This poem without rhyme
is dedicated to the Jewish people
also known as *The Chosen.*

Many generations ago, Moses appeared on Mount Sinai
with the radiance of the Holy Spirit shown from within
while in direct closeness and communion with YHWH.

Moses, a prophet of Judaism, of Christianity,
of Islam and other monotheistic
Abrahamic religions
even after his death, his legacy
serves as the foundation for
The Chosen people
as the basis for living
a just and worthy life
even in the modern-day world.

Likewise, the faith of the Jewish people
is steadfast and everlasting
woven into daily life, literature,
poetry, rituals, and even in
kosher simmering preparations.
All are bonded through the Hebrew language
of many generations.

It is late, and I am still dreaming
of a better world as espoused
in the teachings gathered at
Mount Sinai.

—Ilean Baltodano

Chapter 5

Sephardic and Ashkenazi Jews

Before I begin this chapter, I would like to establish that what I am writing about is nothing new, and my purpose in pursuing this writing project is to explore and share the intricacies of Jewish culture. The information included is based on my research of scholars and eminent writers.

"Sepharad" is the Hebrew name for Spain. *Sephardim* are the Jewish families and/or their descendants who lived in Spain and Portugal from at least the later centuries of the Roman Empire until their persecution and mass expulsion from those countries during the last decade of the fifteenth century. Sephardic Jews lived in the Iberian Peninsula (Spain and Portugal) prior to the Spanish Inquisition. The issuance of the Alhambra Decree, ordered by Queen Isabella I of Castille and King Ferdinand II of Aragon in 1492, forced Spanish Jews to convert to Catholicism or else suffer expulsion from the kingdom.[33]

For a considerable part of the Middle Ages, the Iberian Peninsula—Spain and Portugal, was governed by the Islamic Empire. The Moors invaded the Iberian Peninsula in AD 711, when an African army, under their leader Tariq ibn-Ziyad,[34] crossed the Strait of Gibraltar from Northern Africa. They ruled for eight hundred years, during which philosophy, mathematics, and the sciences—chemistry, physics, geography, and astronomy flourished in Spain.

---

[33] American Historical Association, www.historians.org>Sephardic.

[34] https://en.m.wikipedia.org

The Moors introduced new scientific techniques to Europe, such as a device for measuring the position of the stars and planets. Islam had an important influence on the values and lives of the people, and the Muslims brought much advancement to the European continent.

The Jews especially thrived under Muslim rule from the eighth to the eleventh centuries. The historical record confirms that between the ninth and the eleventh centuries, Joseph ha-Nagid, leader of the Iberian Jews, directly participated in the culture of Spain's famous Alhambra castle in Granada. This period was a time rich in opportunities and possibilities. The Moors and the Jews grew side by side and learned from one another. Jews were free to work as farmers, physicians, astronomers, and diplomats. Hebrew, primarily a language of worship in recent centuries, now in Spain became a language of poetry and songs. In the late fifteenth century, internal feuds and a strengthened Spanish monarchy under Ferdinand and Isabella signaled the downfall of the Moorish civilization in Spain.[35] After the Spanish Inquisition, Spain's Golden Age, "Siglo de Oro" (in Spanish), began about 1500.[36] This epoch lasted for two centuries, until approximately 1680. The marriage of Catholic royals Isabella and Ferdinand V of Castile united the kingdoms of Aragon and Castile, and this Spanish dynasty became the most powerful monarchy in Europe. For two centuries, Spain amassed a mighty empire through conquests and war. The political rise of the Spanish Empire coincided with a period of peace, prosperity, and flourishing in the arts and literature.

During this Spanish Renaissance, El Greco and Velázquez painted their masterpieces, and Cervantes wrote his famous tour de force, *Don Quixote*, often cited as the first modern novel. El Greco was a Greek painter, sculptor, and architect. "El Greco" was actually the nickname of Domenikos Theotokopoulos. The leading painter in the court of King Philip IV of Spain and Portugal was Diego Rodríguez de Silva y Velázquez, better known simply as Velazquez.

---

[35] "The Downfall of the Moorish civilization," https://en.m.wikipedia.org>wiki.

[36] "Golden Age/Siglo de Oro, Spanish Literature and Definition." www.britannica.com>art.

During this period, Jews were generally accepted in society, and the cultural and economic life of the Jewish communities flourished.

The Crusades

The First Crusade was the beginning of several religious wars that Europe's Christian rulers conducted, with the objective of recovering the Holy Land from Islamic rule. The First Crusade began in 1095. Pope Urban II supported this Crusade, which urged Christians to undertake an armed pilgrimage to Jerusalem. Many of the Crusaders saw it as an opportunity to simultaneously serve God and make a fortune by looting and ransom. The Crusaders succeeded in their goals, together with ruthlessly slaughtering the Muslims. As for the Jewish inhabitants in Palestine, they were forced to surrender to the new rulers or face execution. There are accounts of Crusaders— nobles and peasants alike—ruthlessly slaughtering defenseless people and even attacking Jews sheltering in synagogues as they slashed their way through Europe en route to the Holy Land. Thus, the Jews got caught in the Christian quest to recapture the Holy Land from Muslims, and the Crusades affected medieval Jewry in both Europe and Palestine.

The First Crusade initiated an era of persecution of Jews in Germany. During the Black Death, a bubonic plague pandemic, the local population accused the Jews of poisoning the wells. This crisis led to the mass slaughter of German Jews, and those who survived fled in large numbers to Poland. The horror of the First Crusade was not only the lives that were lost but also what was profoundly tragic was the hostility directed against the Jews. The Crusaders victimized the Jewish communities, who were threatened with death if they didn't abandon their Judaism and convert to Christianity. Jews were murdered on the streets. A few agreed to be baptized, but most refused to disprove that their own belief meant more than life itself. Hundreds of Jews committed mass suicide. The Crusades ignited a hostility toward Jews that became an ongoing threat and nightmare.

An estimated 13,000 to 50,000 Jews live in Spain today. As we trace back to the legal basis of a 1924 decree, there have been initiatives to favor the return of Sephardi Jews to Spain by facilitating Spanish citizenship on the basis of demonstrated ancestry. As of 2022, there is Spain's new "grandchildren" citizen law that will allow foreigners with Spanish lineage to get Spanish citizenship.

Famous Sephardim – Sephardic Jews have lived in many countries. They have always brought with them a zest for life and a beautiful culture that is reflected in their creative work. The following list gives examples of but a few of the many famous Sephardic Jews who have positively contributed to the world we live in. From rabbis to doctors and actors to poets, these individuals have changed the direction of both the Jewish and Western world: David Amram, known as "the Renaissance man of American music;" Salvador Edward Luria, born in Italy and won the Nobel Prize in Medicine; Eydie Gorme, Grammy-winning singer and artist; Elias Canetti, born in Bulgaria, Nobel Prize winner in literature; David Ricardo, British economist and one of the most important figures in the development of economic theory; Neil Sedaka, born in New York, composer and rock and roll singer.

The Ashkenazi Jews (plural, Ashkenazim, from Hebrew Ashkenaz, referring to Germany) were a member of the Jewish diaspora and their descendants who lived in the Rhineland valley and in neighboring areas before their migration eastward to Slavic lands (Poland, Lithuania, Russia) after the Crusades of the eleventh to thirteenth centuries.[37] Throughout their numerous centuries living in Europe, Ashkenazim have made many important contributions to Western scholarship in philosophy, literature, art, music, and science.[38] What distinguishes the Ashkenazim from Sephardi Jewry are their cultural traditions, their history of speaking Yiddish, and their Hebrew pronunciation in the synagogue liturgy,[39] including the style of chanting.

About half of Jewish people around the world today identify as Ashkenazi, meaning that they descend from Jews who lived in

---

[37] https://www.britannica.com>topic.
[38] https://en.m.wikipedia.org>wikik.
[39] https://www.britannica.com>What.

Central or Eastern Europe. The term was initially used to define a distinct cultural group of Jews who settled in the Rhineland in western Germany. Albert Einstein, one of the most influential scientists of all time, was an Ashkenazi Jew—as were Gertrude Stein (novelist, poet, playwright, and art collector) and Carl Sagan (astronomer, astrophysicist, author, and professor). Steven Spielberg (film director, producer, and screenwriter) and Scarlett Ingrid Johansson (the world's highest-paid actress in 2018 and 2019) are also Ashkenazi Jews, along with three members of the US Supreme Court—Ruth Bader Ginsburg, Stephen Breyer, and Elena Kagan.

The Ashkenazim and the Sephardim comprise the two major branches of Jewish heritage.

The three caravels

"The ships of Christopher Columbus were sleek, fast—and cramped"[40] is the title of a History Channel online print article that briefly describes his voyage. This story relates, "On August 3, 1492, Christopher Columbus and his crew set sail from the port of Palos in southern Spain on three vessels: la Santa Clara (Niña), la Pinta, and la Santa Gallega (Santa María). Two of the ships, the Niña and Pinta, were tiny by today's standards—only 50 to 70 feet from bow to stern—but prized for their speed and maneuverability. The Santa Maria, Columbus's flagship, was a larger, heavier cargo ship."[41]

<hr>

40   History Channel, https:www.history.com>news.
41   David Roos, "The Ships of Christopher Columbus Were Sleek, Fast and Cramped," July 28, 2023.

Chapter 6

Christopher Columbus—Sail to the Indies and the Jews

For several centuries, the policy *of limpieza* (*cleansing* in Spanish—and perhaps a source of the term *ethnic cleansing*) to the Indies was repeated frequently, and it was directed at Jews, Moors, heretics, new Christians, and other persons penanced by the Inquisition.

> We herewith decree that all the Jews living in our dominions, without distinction of sex and age, must leave our royal possessions and seigneuries, together with their sons and daughters and their Jewish servants…and let them not presume to set foot again in the land for the purpose of settlement, or to pass through to some other land, or for any purpose whatsoever.
>
> Royal Edict of Expulsion: By midnight, August 2, 1492, all Jews must leave Spanish soil.[42]

Coincidentally, Christopher Columbus was determined to find a route to India, China, Japan, and also the Spice Islands—a small group of islands to the northeast of Indonesia. His goal was to

---

[42] Simon Wiesenthal, Sails of Hope: The Secret Mission of Christopher Columbus (New York: MacMillan Publishing Co. Inc., 1973).

bring back rich cargoes of silks and spices. Columbus was an Italian explorer and navigator from the Republic of Genoa, a Mediterranean coastal region of northwest Italy near France. While he initially was in search of a westward route to the Indies, his four transatlantic maritime expeditions led to the discovery of the Americas.

The Spanish and Portuguese crowns issued decrees whereby Jews were excluded from society. Jews and converted Jews (Christian Jews) were prohibited by law from entering the colonial dependencies of Spain; thus, considering the pressures exerted on them, it would not be surprising if some of them looked abroad for new lands where they could live in peace. Furthermore, in regard to these circumstances, there is yet another theory that "Spanish Conversos" (Christian Jews) were involved in the discovery of the New World. Some theorists believe that the discovery of America and the expulsion of the Jews are the two events that had the most far-reaching consequences for the entire course of Spanish history.

According to one study, "Auspicious coincidence of these two events—compounded with the intense mystery which has always surrounded the identity of Columbus—has led to a complete reexamination of all previously accepted theories about the true nature of his mission."[43]

The first voyage Columbus made to the East Indies (what we today know as Southwest Asia) began on the night of August 2, 1492, which is when, per order by Columbus, all the members of the expedition were required to be on board. However, we know that the three caravels were not put to sea until the next day, August 3. It was customary for sailors to linger at the port with their families until very shortly before a ship was due to sail. Thus, it is curious that Columbus insisted his crew be on the ship the day before.

> That same night, the three sailing ships…
> are anchored quietly in Palos Harbor—and
> although they are not scheduled to embark until
> the following day, Columbus has ordered his

---

[43] Simon Wiesenthal, Sails of Hope: The Secret Mission of Christopher Columbus (New York: MacMillan Publishing Co. Inc., 1973), 4.

crew to be on board by eleven o'clock that night. A Hebrew translator, Luis de Torres, will accompany the expedition, but strangely enough, not a single priest is included.[44]

Let's hear from Columbus himself, from his journal:

> After you, Holy Kings, expelled the Jews from your lands in the same month of January, Your Majesties sent me with a fleet to the Lands of the Indies.[45]

Could there have been Jews on Columbus's ships? Might there be a connection between his voyage of discovery and the expulsion of the Jews? Research reveals an interesting theory that Columbus was of Jewish origin and that his 1492 voyage was actually a desperate search for a new homeland for the Jews. According to Simon Wiesenthal:

> The Edict of Expulsion was signed on March 31, 1492, whereas Columbus's voyage was approved three months before, in January— although the contract between Columbus and the two sovereigns was not signed until April 17. Thus, dates come together: January, Columbus's voyage is approved; March, Edict of Expulsion; August 2 last day for the Jews to remain legally in Spain, coinciding with the eve of Columbus's departure.[46]

On August 3, 1492, Columbus started his voyage across the Atlantic Ocean. He and his crew set sail from Spain in three ships

---

44 Simon Wiesenthal, Sails of Hope: The Secret Mission of Christopher Columbus (New York: MacMillan Publishing Co. Inc., 1973), 4.

45 Simon Wiesenthal, Sails of Hope: The Secret Mission of Christopher Columbus (New York: MacMillan Publishing Co. Inc., 1973), 4.

46 Simon Wiesenthal, Sails of Hope: The Secret Mission of Christopher Columbus (New York: MacMillan Publishing Co. Inc., 1973), 4.

called caravels. They were small, light, fast-sailing ships of the time, much used by the Spanish and Portuguese for long voyages during the fifteenth to the seventeenth centuries. Spanish ships were traditionally named after saints and usually given nicknames. These three caravels had interesting names: The *Niña* (the Girl), the *Pinta* (the Painted One or the Spotted One), and the *Santa Maria* (the Saint Mary). The *Niña* and the *Pinta* were tiny by today's standards. The *Pinta* was the fastest. The *Santa Maria* was a larger, heavier cargo ship.

Could it be that there were mostly Jews in the three caravels? It is intriguing that Columbus was financed by Jewish lenders. His expedition was not, as is commonly believed, funded by the deep pockets of Queen Isabella but rather by two Jewish Conversos and another prominent Jew. Louis de Santangel and Gabriel Sanchez advanced an interest-free loan of 17,000 ducats from their own pockets to help pay for the voyage, as did Don Isaac Abarbanel, rabbi and Jewish statesman.[47]

According to the book *The Log of Christopher Columbus* by Robert Fuson, Columbus altered his identity, hiding many facts from his own sons. Columbus's son Fernando wrote in his memoir that his father elected to leave in obscurity everything pertaining to his birthplace and family. It seems that Columbus is "a riddle wrapped in a mystery inside an enigma" (to borrow a phrase from Winston Churchill). Fuson asserts that:

> At almost every turn of the maze, there is an obstruction. When was Columbus born? We are not sure. The year 1441 is usually given, sometimes between August 25 and October 31. But some have placed it as early as 1435 and others as late as 1460. Columbus made conflicting statements concerning the date. Nor do we know for certain where he was born.[48]

---

[47] Don Isaac Abarbanel, Rabbi and Jewish statesman, writes 2012 CNN article, "Was Columbus Secretly a Jew?"

[48] Robert H. Fuson, *The Log of Christopher Columbus* (Camden, Maine: International Marine Publishing Co., 1987), 13.

But why all the secrecy? First, there may have been a political reason. Second, there may have been a religious reason. There is abundant circumstantial evidence that Columbus had a Jewish background, at least on one side of the family. Salvador de Madariaga and Simon Wiesenthal, in *Sails of Hope: The Secret Mission of Christopher Columbus,* have provided more than enough documentation to convince any objective person. This does not mean that Columbus was anything less than a devout Christian. In fifteenth-century Spain, a convert or the descendant of a convert did not boast of Jewish ancestry. This was something kept within a very tight circle of friends and often only within the family.

Another interesting theory presented about Columbus is that he was not, as portrayed by history, of a humble background, but instead, as reflected by his sophisticated personal library, he was very well educated and possessed an uncommonly broad knowledge of languages, history, geography, and the Bible. His reading notes point to a surprising knowledge of Hebrew lore. He was also an expert cartographer—a profession practiced at that time almost exclusively by Jews.

Moreover, there may have been a family reason. Was Columbus really the son of poor wool weavers? How did he acquire his considerable education? How could a commoner and a foreign one, no less, marry into the Portuguese nobility? How was Columbus able to move among royalty as a peer? Was the admiral of higher birth than many suppose?[49]

A corroboration of Columbus's Jewish roots is offered by a daily bulletin of the 1934 Jewish Telegraphic Agency:

> The help afforded him by Jewish scientists and financiers of that time can be explained only in the light that he was of the same race, the writer concluded and cited the 1892 work, Columbus and his Discovery of America, in which Herbert B. Adams wrote: "Not jewels, but Jews were the real financial basis for the first expedition of Columbus."[50]

---

[49] Robert H. Fuson, *The Log of Christopher Columbus* (Camden, Maine: International Marine Publishing Co., 1987), 14–22.

[50] Herbert Baxter Adams and Ellen Wood, *Columbus and His Discovery of America.*

At the same time, historian Aliza Moreno-Goldschmidt claims, "The truth is that in the scholarly world, it's not very accepted [to say] he was a Jew. I tend to believe he was not." Another reason that Columbus gets a lot of bad press in recent times is the popularity of the current anti-colonialist theory, which argues that Columbus:

> Opened the way for European countries to colonize and exploit the lands and their people... [and] paved the way for the slave trade between Europe, Africa, and the Americas. They brought with them diseases that had a devastating effect on Native American populations. Many native people perished or were driven from their home by colonizers.[51]

Columbus was sure that he had reached the Indies. He called all the people he met in America *Indians*. This initial encounter opened up the *New World* to European colonization, which would come to have a devastating impact on indigenous populations. Even though Columbus never stepped foot on the mainland of North America,[52] the Columbus Day holiday has come under fire as a celebration of a man whose arrival in the Americas heralded the oppression of Native Americans. Therefore, in recent decades, this day has been renamed in many states and cities as *Indigenous Peoples Day*.[53]

Nevertheless, even though the theory of the secret Jewish heritage of Columbus has not gained wide acceptance among historians, *his voyages bear strong Jewish overtones, from the identities of some crew members, key conversos in the Spanish court, and the pattern of scientific inquiry that helped make the voyage possible.*[54]

---

[51] Editors of Encyclopedia Britannica.

[52] https://www.rmg.co.uk.

[53] Nationalgeographic.com.

[54] *Jews and the Americas* (Brown University), https://brown.edu>geography+.

Concentration camps

From 1933 to 1945, Nazi Germany and its allies established more than 44,000 camps and other incarceration sites (including ghettos). The perpetrators used these sites for a range of purposes, including forced labor, detention of people thought to be enemies of the state, and mass murder.[55]

---

[55] Holocaust Encyclopedia, Camp System: Maps.

Chapter 7

The Holocaust

The Second World War took the lives of sixty million people; more than six million of them were exterminated through crimes so atrocious that a new name to describe them was coined: *the Holocaust.*[56] Although there were courageous individuals who risked everything to save Jews from the Nazis, two-thirds of the entire global Jewish population was decimated.

Anti-Semitism is hatred or prejudice directed against Jews. It is a form of discrimination. Anti-Semitism has existed since the time of the early Christian church until the present day. It has been documented throughout the Middle Ages, in the twentieth century, and in the current twenty-first century. Unfortunately, genocide did not begin or end with the Holocaust. Prejudice, discrimination, and even genocide can be found throughout history in all parts of the world. Sometimes discrimination is camouflaged by anti-immigrant and anti-minority views, often expressed by an attitude of "we don't want those who are different from us."

Holocaust denial is a form of anti-Semitism that attempts to negate the established facts of the Nazi genocide of European Jewry. Some people might not be overtly antisemitic but are discomforted with the idea of Jews as victims. Unfortunately, this attitude is currently on the rise in the United States, as evident in slogans such as "the Holocaust is fake history" and new stories of extremists attacking synagogues.

---

[56] "The Holocaust/The National WWII Museum/New Orleans," www.nationalww2museum.org

I believe that we are a connected global community, and this attitude should not be tolerated. We all should stand together as a family. According to the executive director of Anne Frank House, Ronald Leopold, "Over the long term, education and information are the best answers to the question of how anti-Semitism can be countered effectively."

In addition to Nazi concentration camps, prison camps in modern times have included Stalin's gulags and have been seen in Cuba, South Africa, and North Korea.[57] We have the example and testimony of Shin Dong-hyuk, who was born in a political prison camp in North Korea, escaped to China, and made his way to South Korea in 2006. He lived in the United States for two years before returning to South Korea, where he became a human rights activist. Most recently, the Uyghurs in China have been incarcerated, harassed, and tortured.

In 1933, Franklin Delano Roosevelt was inaugurated president, and Adolf Hitler was named Chancellor of Germany. Within half a year, the life of every single Jew living in Germany was radically changed. Parks are designed for public use and enjoyment, but during the war years, messages such as "No Jews in the parks" started to circulate. Jewish children were stoned on the way to school. This was the beginning of the dominion of hell.

Through secret meetings, missionaries from the United States started training to do missionary work abroad. They learned the technique of writing memos that could not be easily deciphered, memorized key words and important data, including methods of destroying incriminating papers, as well as how to ascertain if they were shadowed, and many more strategies. All these practices were in the hope of saving Jews and others who were in danger of being deported to the camps.

In 1939, Hitler occupied Czechoslovakia. Due to the foreign exchange crisis,[58] Germany decided to seize the gold of the Czechoslovak central bank. Following the Nazis occupation, Jews

---

[57] "Concentration Camps History," www.smithsonianmag.com
[58] "Occupation of Czechoslovakia (1938–1945), Wikipedia,

were persecuted in all parts of Czechoslovakia. However, at this point in time, life in the United States was pretty secure, and most Americans weren't paying attention to what was happening overseas.

In 1940, Hitler invaded France. Germany cut off basic supplies to the South of France, such as meat, fruits, vegetables, and powdered milk for infants. The French, along with Belgians and foreigners, were affected by the occupation, and some fled to southern Europe. Those assisting the Jews to evacuate decided that the only possible way to do so was to get them out illegally.

President Roosevelt (FDR) was subsequently reelected and then elected again to unprecedented third and fourth terms. Throughout his long presidency, his wife, First Lady Eleanor Roosevelt, was known as "the president's eyes, ears, and legs." Many Jews appealed to the First Lady. Sadly, allowing refugees to enter the country was difficult due to the quota system. President Roosevelt lacked support to challenge Congress. Nevertheless, Eleanor used her social and political influence to intervene on behalf of the refugees. The Wagner-Rogers Bill[59] was supposed to permit the entry of 20,000 German refugee children, ages fourteen and under, into the United States over the course of two years. Eleonor told reporters this bill was "a wise way to do a humanitarian act." But unfortunately, the bill died in committee.

In June, Eleanor formed a committee to coordinate rescue efforts for the children. By 1943, the committee succeeded in rescuing several hundred Jewish children from Western Europe. Many children were saved and brought to America. It was heartbreaking, no doubt, for parents to hand their children off to strangers. There is a tendency to think that you can protect your children by holding them close and keeping them in your arms. But in certain circumstances, that instinctive reaction may not be the wise one. Even though lives were saved, the rescue effort had devastating effects. The young ones were traumatized by having to adapt to a new life, a new language, and many more sudden changes subsequent to separation from their parents.

---

[59] Wagner-Roger Bill/Holocaust Encyclopedia, https://encyclopedia.ushmn.org.

I am reminded of how the Hebrew Bible mentions the mother of Moses, Jochebed (pronounced *Yocheved* in Hebrew), looking desperately for a way to save her newborn son after Pharaoh ordered the killing of all the firstborn male babies. "*She hid him in a basket made of reeds and left him on the riverbed,*"[60] knowing that Pharaoh's daughter came to bathe there. Jochebed's action saved her son Moses and thus prepared him for the salvation of the oppressed Israelites in Egypt.

In 1940, the German authorities established a ghetto in the capital city of Poland. In one book about the Warsaw Ghetto, *The Chronicle of the Courageous Heart of Irena Sendler*, we can learn some of the history of what happened to the 460,000 Jews who were trapped there. Thousands of Jews disappeared within the Warsaw Ghetto. A few of the Polish people risked their lives to save Jewish children. Many children were placed with Catholic families and in farms and Christian convents. Even though they might be raised as Christians, parents were willing to do whatever they could to rescue their children to safety. As a Polish social worker, Irena Sendler had access to the ghetto and was able to save approximately 2,500 Jewish children during the German occupation. Even when the Gestapo eventually captured and tortured Irena, she refused to divulge any information about her work and the Jewish families she helped. Irena Sendler was one of the most remarkable heroes of WWII. Here is what she said in a speech she gave after the war:

> Not so long ago, it was Mother's Day. So, today, I would like us to celebrate this holiday in the name of some of the most anguished mothers in the world, the Jewish mothers who had to part with their children during those terrible times. And let us reflect on those Polish women who took the Jewish children in and brought them up as their own, risking their lives every day and every hour. They loved those children so much that when the war ended, they could hardly bear to part. So let us give thought to those mothers.

---

[60] Exodus 2.

In 2007, Irena Sendler was honored with a nomination for the Nobel Peace Prize. She died in May of 2008 in Warsaw, Poland. She was ninety-eight years old.

Another heroic Gentile was Oskar Schindler,[61] a German industrialist who saved more than a thousand Polish Jews. Schindler did something extraordinary by employing the refugees in his factory during WWII. His factory was a haven. In April of 1944, Department D gave orders to exhume and incinerate the bodies of more than 10,000 Jews killed at the Kraków-Plaszów Nazi concentration camp in Poland. This was when Schindler began saving the lives of his factory workers. He spent millions of Reichsmarks to sustain his workers and bribe Reich officials. (The Reichsmark was the monetary unit of the Third Reich, replaced in 1948 by the Deutschmark.) Schindler's munitions factory became intentionally nonproductive. Itzhak Stern was the Polish Jew who worked for Oskar Schindler as his accountant and assisted him in the rescue activities, which included typing the list of names of individuals, now employees of Schindler's factory, who were being rescued.

Schindler's List, the Stephen Spielberg film that brought this story to public attention, was based on a book by Australian author Thomas Keneally, who wrote *Oskar Schindler's Ark* in 1982.[62] Keneally's book is a novelized version of the actual history of what occurred, as reported to him by a number of rescued persons, and the narrative is based primarily on interviews with these Holocaust survivors located in seven countries—Australia, Israel, West Germany, Austria, the United States, Argentina, and Brazil.

Near the end of the *Schindler's List* film, we encounter this gripping scene:

> (Clacking sound of a mechanical typewriter)
> As the Accountant Stern types, Schindler asks,
> "How many names?"
> Stern replies, "Four hundred fifty names."

---

[61] Listed under Bibliography/Books and Films.
[62] Under Bibliography/Books.

Schindler insists: "Type more…more…more names!"
(We see some of the names: Ludmila Pfefferberg, Helen Horowitz, Jonas Dresner, Rebecca Bau, Leopold Rosner…and names of Jewish investors, children's names, and many more.)
Schindler asks again, "How many names?"
Stern replies, "Eight hundred fifty names, give or take…"
Schindler demands: "More…more…type…more names!"

Next, we hear the voice of Winston Churchill on the radio announcing that the Act of Unconditional Surrender of all German land, sea, and air forces in Europe to the Allied expeditionary forces and simultaneously to the Soviet High Command was signed at General Eisenhower's headquarters. The German war was at an end.

Schindler addresses his Jewish workers:

> At midnight tonight, the war will be over. Tomorrow, you'll begin the process of looking for survivors of your families. In most cases, you won't find them. After six long years of murder, victims are being mourned throughout the world. Many of you have come up to me and thanked me. Thank yourselves! I am a member of the Nazi Party. I am a munitions manufacturer. I am a profiteer of slave labor. I am a criminal. At midnight, you'll be free, and I'll be hunted. I hope you'll forgive me. I have to flee [sighs].

Response from Jewish employees:

> We've written a letter trying to explain things in case you are captured.

Every worker signed it. They gave him a ring scripted in Hebrew from the Talmud: "Whoever saves one life, saves the world entire."

One thousand one hundred people were alive and saved from certain death because of Oskar Schindler. There will be generations of descendants because of his courageous efforts. In 1958, Oskar Schindler was declared a "Righteous Person" by the council of YAD VASHEM of the Israeli Parliament, and he was invited to plant a tree in the Avenue of the Righteous. There are now more than six thousand descendants of the Schindler Jews.

Another great model of rescue is the immigration project of Waitstill and Martha Sharp. In December of 1941, the United States was finally forced to join the war that had been raging in Europe and Asia for more than two years. All through the war, Waitstill and Martha Sharp continued their efforts to help rescue refugees. In June 2006, the State of Israel awarded Martha and Waitstill Sharp the highest honor of "Righteous among the Nations." This is Israel's highest award, and it has been bestowed on 27,000 individuals who risked their lives to save Jews from extermination during the Holocaust. The Sharps are two of only five Americans (as of 2022) who have received this recognition: Varian Fry, Lois Gunden, Roddie Edmonds, Waitstill Sharp, and Martha Sharp. This recognition was also awarded to Raoul Wallenberg, Diplomat Aristides de Souza Mendes, the Italian cycling champion Gino Bartali, and the Japanese spy Chiune Sugihara. These heroes provided hiding places, participated in underground networks, refused to betray their neighbors, and secured safe passage to save the persecuted.

Tova Friedman is one of the youngest survivors of Auschwitz and uses her vivid memories in *The Daughter of Auschwitz* to speak against anti-Semitism and prejudice. Tova's memories remind readers of the horrors of the Holocaust at a time when hate is on the rise around the world.

For twelve years (1933–1945), Adolf Hitler held Germany in an iron grip. Operation D-Day was the largest seaborne invasion in history. D-Day *marked the turn of the tide for the control maintained by Nazi Germany.*[63] Just two weeks after the D-Day landing in

---

[63] "Normandy Landings: June 6, 1944," https://en.m.wikipedia.org/wiki/D-Day.

Normandy, a top secret team of British agents considered an alternate plan to end the war more quickly. Operation Foxley was an audacious plot to murder Adolf Hitler. He ruled absolutely *until his death by suicide in April 1945.* The fate of history lies in the hands of humanity to demonstrate faithfulness to the ideals of freedom, tolerance, anti-immigrant sentiments, respect for people from all different backgrounds, and peace in the world.

The Holocaust Happened!

This is a harsh reality,
an incomprehensible chapter in history.
Let's fight anti-Semitism,
hostility, prejudice, and bigotry.

Listen, new generation, children,
Grandchildren, and great-grandchildren:
The Holocaust happened.
The gas chambers happened.

The survivor's sentiment
is sad and tragic.
New generations, be aware.
There is good and evil in the world.

Let's fight for the helpless.
Let's teach humanity to the inhumane.
Let's destroy the powerful evil.
Let's fight for honesty and reverence.

Let's not forget,
The Holocaust happened!
But we can overcome hate with love.

—Ilean Baltodano

Chapter 8

Jews Who Settled in the Americas

First, allow me to briefly touch on history and the names of two individuals, Amerigo Vespucci and Gerardus Mercator. But who was Amerigo? Did he really journey to South America before his famous friend Christopher Columbus did? And why do two of the world's continents bear his name? In the book *Forgotten Voyager: The Story of Amerigo Vespucci*, Ann Fitzpatrick Alper presents a convincing account of what may have been.

Back in the sixteenth century, Amerigo Vespucci, an Italian explorer, cartographer, and navigator from the Republic of Florence, was the first European to suggest that the Americas were not part of the East Indies—but that this was an entirely separate landmass.[64] Vespucci was in his forties when he decided to embark on a journey. The period in which he made his voyages under Spanish auspices fell between 1497 and 1504. He verified the status of what came to be called the New World by following the coast of South America down to the southernmost tip of South America, which Magellan a few years later named *Tierra del Fuego* ("Fireland" in English).

The name America was literally put on the map by the cartographer Gerardus Mercator. He was well known for creating in 1569 the world map where he applied the name *America*. He also introduced the term *atlas* for a bound collection of maps.

---

[64] Ann Fitzpatrick, *Forgotten Voyager: The Story of Amerigo Vespucci* (Minneapolis: Carolrhoda Books Inc., 1991), 57.

However, while it is generally accepted that the designation *America* derives from the name of Italian sailor Amerigo Vespucci, who explored the new continent on behalf of Spain and Portugal, some scholars have suggested other explanations. It has been suggested that America is named after the Amerrisque Mountains in Nicaragua or perhaps after Richard Amerike, a Bristol, English businessman, because his coat of arms, with its stars and stripes pattern, was similar to the flag later adopted by the independent United States of America.

There is so much left to question about the legendary, and to some, infamous *discoverer* of America, Christopher Columbus. Was he secretly a Jew? Was he a convert or the descendant of a convert? Where and when was he born? What exactly is the year of his birth? Is it 1435? Is it 1441? Or could it be 1460? His given name when he was born was Cristoforo Colombo. He was not, as portrayed by history, of a humble background. His personal papers exhibit a surprising knowledge of Hebrew lore. And he was an expert cartographer—at that time, a profession practiced almost exclusively by Jews. Could his 1492 voyage have been a desperate search for a new homeland for the Jews?

Arguments about his origins and final resting place are the subject of controversy. Both Seville, Spain, and Santo Domingo, in the Dominican Republic, claim to have his remains. What is the historical truth regarding Christopher Columbus? His son Ferdinand tells of an obscure fact about his father. It seems that Columbus, thinking he had missed China and reached the Indian Ocean, found the islands that he named the West Indies. On his third voyage, in 1498, he landed on the mainland of South America.

Of course, we now know that neither Columbus nor John Cabot—an Italian who sailed under the English flag and reached Newfoundland in 1497—was the first explorer or European to arrive in America. Native Americans had crossed the Bering Strait from Asia in prehistoric times, migrating south and becoming, in time, American Indians, Mayans, Olmecs, Aztecs, and Incas. Moreover, research reveals that Vikings set off from the west coast of Greenland nearly 500 years before Columbus and landed on the shores of North America.

Until the Age of Exploration, the Europeans were unaware of the existence of the American continents. So in what sense did the colonial empires *discover* America? *Discovery* is *an act or the process of finding someone or something or learning about something that was not known about before.* Thus, the discovery of America was simply the perception of the explorers and the colonial lands from which they embarked to reach the New World.

The majority of Jews who came to America were from Europe, although many took themselves and their traditions all over the world. Those who arrived in the New World before the twentieth century were technically illegal immigrants who were risking their lives if they were caught. Nevertheless, Jewish communities were under such intense pressure in Europe that many Jews fled to the Americas, where the opportunity for anonymity was considerably greater than at home. In the years 1820 through 1924, a steady flow of Jews made their way to America, urged by economic hardship, persecution, and the great social and political disturbances denying their freedom and restricting their rights.

Most Jewish immigrants were Ashkenazi Jews from Central and Eastern Europe who arrived in large numbers after 1889. Perhaps a tenth of Jewish immigrants were Sephardic Jews from North Africa, Turkey, and the Balkans, whose ancestors hailed from Spain and Portugal. Their traditional language is Ladino, which is a dialect of Spanish. Thus, it is not surprising that large numbers of Sephardim chose to seek a new homeland in Latin America. For these groups of immigrants who settled in Central and South America, the process of assimilation into the new culture was less facile than it was for Jews who landed in North America.

The difference between the experience of Jews who settled in South America and those who settled in the United States is discussed by Judith Laikin Elkin. Her book, *Jews of the Latin American Republics,* presents an insightful chapter comparing Jewish life in the United States with Jewish life in the Latin American republics. Although Jewish immigrants assimilated quickly on both continents, in Latin America, they found themselves marginalized by key institutions such as the army, the church, aristocracy, and radical groupings. Although many Latin American Jewish families prospered economically, they were frustrated in their efforts to become fully participating citizens. The impermeability of Latin American social institutions challenged the ability of a non-Latin, non-Catholic minority to enjoy complete success.

Many Latin American Jews, despite their skills as economic innovators, occupied a precarious position in national politics. Their traditional vulnerability on religious grounds was intensified by economic and political pressures within national societies where cultural pluralism has not been a vital ideal.

In *The Tango War*, Mary Jo McConahay describes how WWII was a global war. There was a need to control not just the hearts and minds but also the resources of Latin America. It was called a tango war, in which each side closely shadowed the other's steps. This was not only about the arrival of the Jews in America. *The Tango War* describes the machinations behind the greatest mass flight of criminals of the century—the fascists with blood on their hands desperately escaping from the legal authorities to a wished-for new identity and fresh start in the Americas.

For a good overview of the status of the Jewish diaspora in Latin America, one excellent resource is Judith Laikin Elkin's book. *Jews of the Latin American Republics* is a comprehensive study of South and Central American Jewry in modern times. It extends our present knowledge of the demographics and ethnic composition of Latin American populations and portrays the Latin American diaspora as a separate branch of world Jewry. Elkin's study begins with a discussion of the status of Jews and conversos in the Iberian empires. A review of the great global migrations of Jews in the nineteenth and twentieth centuries establishes the origins and motivations of those who settled in Latin America. Elkin places their arrival in the context of policies relating to immigrant recruitment, economic development, and religious toleration in each republic. She argues that this interaction between immigrant and host society determined the course of Jewish life on the continent.

One individual whose life exemplifies some of the obstacles of living as a Jew in South America is Jacobo Timerman, who was born in 1923 in the Ukrainian town of Bar, then part of the Soviet Union. His family arrived in Argentina in 1928. He became a lifelong journalist. In the 1960s, he founded two weekly news magazines and was a prominent news commentator on radio and television. His book, *Prisoner without a Name, Cell without a Number,* shares the horrifying story of his arrest, imprisonment, interrogation, and torture before a worldwide campaign won him his freedom in the fall of 1979. He was held captive for thirty months and barbarously tortured and interrogated about his participation in Zionist organizations and his loyalty to Argentina. The book relates how he managed, through his sure sense of identity and by a calculated passivity, to preserve his strength in spite of torment that invited breakdown or madness. And he describes the irrational anti-Semitism of some Argentine officials; pictures of Hitler were hung in rooms where Jewish political prisoners were questioned. This is a magnificent testament, a deeply moving memoir of a brave man's triumph over the mindless brutality and repression of an authoritarian society. Mr. Timerman and his family now live in Tel Aviv, Israel.

In Latin America, the epithets of *Jew* and *devil* became synonymous because the Spaniards transmitted many negative rumors about Jewish people. Some Spanish dictionaries contained defamatory definitions of Jews. Even today, the term Jew is considered offensive in some Central American countries, and the term Israelite is used instead.

Historical facts reveal that the contemporary Jewish communities of Latin America were formed between 1889 and World War II. The reasons for immigration were threefold: the horror they experienced forced them to flee, international travel was relatively cheap, and most countries of the western hemisphere had unrestricted immigration policies.

Latin America

The history of the Jews in Latin America began with *conversos,* who joined the Spanish and Portuguese expeditions to the continents. The Alhambra Decree of 1492 led to the mass conversion of Spain's Jews to Catholicism and the expulsion of those Jews who refused conversion. However, most conversos were prevented from leaving Spain due to Spain's *Blood Statutes* that required all persons traveling to the New World to provide written documentation of Old Christian lineage. This was a racially discriminatory term used in the Spanish and Portuguese Empires during the early modern era to identify those "proper" Christians by virtue of not having Muslim or Jewish ancestors. Those *conversos* stranded in Spain gradually assimilated into their Catholic cultural environment.

Nevertheless, the first Jews came with Columbus on his first expedition. Among them was Spanish sailor Rodrigo de Triana, believed to be the first European from the Age of Exploration to have seen the Americas, and Luis de Torres, who was Columbus' interpreter on his first voyage to America. De Torres was a *converso,* chosen by Columbus for his knowledge of Hebrew and Arabic.[65]

Central America

Guatemala: From the mid-nineteenth to the mid-twentieth century, Jews arrived from Germany and Eastern Europe, beginning with Polish families who settled in Guatemala City and Quetzaltenango. Early in the twentieth century, continuing through WWII, Jews arrived from Turkey and several other locations in the Middle East. Most of the 900 or so Jews there today live in Guatemala City.[66]

Belize: A trading place for Jews of Jamaica. In 1939, during WWII, eighty-five British Jews managed to escape and get to Belize.[67]

---

[65] "History of First Jews in Latin America," https://en.wikipedia.org>wiki.

[66] "History of First Jews in Guatemala," https://en.m.wikipedia.org>wiki.

[67] "History of First Jews in Belize," http://jewswerehere.com>central.

El Salvador: Jews have been present in El Salvador since the early nineteenth century, starting with Sephardic Jews and continuing with the arrival of refugees from Europe during WWII.[68]

Honduras: The arrival of European Jews began between 1920 and 1940. The majority of Jews who arrived in Honduras were Ashkenazis of German, Polish, and Romanian origin fleeing Europe due to the onset of WWII.[69]

Nicaragua: It is likely that Jews first arrived in Nicaragua during the Spanish colonization of the Americas as part of a wave of *conversos* fleeing the Spanish Inquisition. Besides conversos, one of the first Jewish families to immigrate to Nicaragua was the Oppenheimers, originally from France.[70]

Costa Rica: The first Sephardic Jews arrived in colonial times and settled in the colonial capital Cartago and its surroundings. The largest migration of Sephardic Jews occurred in the nineteenth century from Panama, Jamaica, Curaçao, and Saint Thomas, the majority prospering in trade.[71]

Panama: The history of the Jews in Panama can be traced back to the 1500s when the first Crypto-Jewish Sephardi immigrants began to arrive from Spain and Portugal. Crypto-Judaism is the secret adherence to Judaism while publicly professing to be of another faith. Panama has the largest Jewish population in Central America. Panama is the only country (not including Israel) to have had as many as three Jewish presidents during the twentieth century.[72]

The Caribbean

The Caribbean is home to thirteen islands. It is thought that the Jewish presence in the Caribbean began in 1530 with Jews fleeing the Spanish Inquisition.[73]

---

[68] "History of First Jews in El Salvador," https://en.m.wikipedia.org/wiki/His.

[69] "History of First Jews in Honduras," https://en.m.wikipedia.org>wiki.

[70] "History of First Jews in Nicaragua," https://www.jewishvirtuallibrary.org>.

[71] "History of First Jews in Costa Rica, https://en.m.wikipedia.org>wiki.

[72] "History of the Jews in Panama," https://en.m.wikipedia.org>wiki.

[73] "History of the Jews in Latin America and the Caribbean," https://en.m.wikipedia.org.

South America

The Jewish presence in South America is made up mostly of Ashkenazi descendants of Jews who left Germany, Eastern Europe, and Russia. Sephardic Jews, descendants of Jews from Spain and Portugal, form a minority of the Jewish population in South America. The Kahal Zur Israel Synagogue in Recife, Brazil,[74] was founded in 1636 and was the first synagogue in the Americas.

The United States

In the first half of the nineteenth century, Jewish immigrants came from Central Europe, settling in New York, Philadelphia, and Baltimore. Groups of German-speaking Jews made their way to Cincinnati, Albany, Cleveland, Louisville, Minneapolis, St. Louis, New Orleans, San Francisco, and dozens of small towns across the United States.[75]

> So prominent was the Jewish role
> in the foreign commerce of Europe
> that those nations that received the Jews gained
> and the countries that excluded them
> lost in the volume of international trade.[76]
> —Will Durant (American historian and philosopher)

---

[74] "Kahal Zur Israel Synagogue," https://en.m.wikipedia.org>wiki.

[75] "History of the Jews in the United States," https://en.m.wikipedia.org.

[76] Will Durant quote, https://quotefancy.com>quote>Wikipedia.

Chapter 9

Jews Who Made History

History is the study of past events, particularly in human affairs.[77] The continuing legacy of Jewish Americans is well known. Jewish history has included periods of intense migration. As a result of centuries of anti-Semitism that resulted in discrimination, persecution, and genocide, the Jewish people have learned resilience. Jewish culture has changed the world with the contributions of its members to the larger society. Following are a few names of Jewish individuals who have made history:

Moses[78] (thirteenth and fourteenth century BCE) – the most important Jewish prophet in the Bible. He is a key figure of biblical history who led the Jewish people from slavery in Egypt across the Red Sea to the promised land. He received and wrote down the Ten Commandments. Several major world religions believe that God gave Moses the Ten Commandments on Mount Sinai—the ten rules on how people should live and behave. The Ten Commandments of Judaism and Christianity are known as the Decalogue ("ten words" in Greek).[79]

Albert Einstein[80] (1879–1955) – theoretical physicist and Nobel Prize winner. He is one of the few scientists whose name is instantly recognizable worldwide. Plenty of people have heard of

---

[77] Definition from Oxford Languages.

[78] https://www.britannica.com>Moses-Hebrew-prophet.

[79] "Moses," World History Encyclopedia, https://www.worldhistory.org.

[80] https://www.britannica.com>Moses-Hebrew-prophet.

him, but his work is not easy to understand. Einstein was born in southern Germany. His father was an electrical engineer and owned a company making electrical instruments and equipment. Young Albert was not an exceptional student at school. His uncle helped him in mathematics, and his mother encouraged him in literature and music. In his teens, he began to excel in higher mathematics. At the time, science was very popular in Germany. Many inventions, including the motorcycle and the automobile, were being made by German engineers—pioneers in their field.

Einstein became recognized in the scientific world for four landmark papers in 1905, the year he earned his PhD, which he received in January 1906. He became a lecturer at the University of Berlin and then an associate professor of physics in Zurich. For his work in theoretical physics, he received the Nobel Prize in 1922. Einstein's theories have led to a better understanding of the way the universe works—from the force of gravity we feel on Earth to the movements of the stars and planets through space and time.

During the 1920s, Einstein continued to speak out against Germany's political and military aims. When Adolf Hitler and the Nazis came to power in 1933, Einstein and his wife fled to Belgium, then to England, and finally to the United States to accept a position at Princeton University, where he remained based for the rest of his life.

He did not use his fame to seek great power or wealth. Instead, he lived a quiet life and enjoyed music and sailing. During his later years, he campaigned for an end to all nuclear weapons. He was a keen supporter of the movement to establish an independent Jewish homeland with the creation of the state of Israel. In 1952, Einstein was offered the position of president of Israel, but he declined. When he died in Princeton in 1955, the world knew that it had lost one of the greatest scientific minds of all time. Many have heard of his most famous equation of $E=mc^2$. Energy = mass times (the square of) the speed of light.[81]

---

[81] Steve Parker, Albert Einstein and Relativity (New York-Philadelphia: Chelsea House Publishers, 1995).

> The most beautiful emotion we can experience is the mysterious. It is the fundamental emotion that stands at the cradle of all true art and science. He to whom this emotion is a stranger, who can no longer wonder and stand rapt in awe, is as good as dead, a snuffed-out candle. To sense that behind anything that can be experienced there is something that our minds cannot grasp, whose beauty and sublimity reaches us only indirectly: this is religiousness. In this sense, and in this sense only, I am a devoutly religious man.[82] (Albert Einstein)

Irving Berlin[83] (1888–1989) – the immigrant boy who made America sing. He arrived in the United States at the age of five. Irving stood on tiptoe to see over the handrail around the deck of the ship. Behind him, too far to glimpse, was Russia, where angry Cossacks had burned his family's home to ashes. Ahead was America. The Statue of Liberty seemed to welcome them. "God bless America," his mother said. One day, Irving promised himself, "I am going to write a song just for her."

The son of a cantor, Berlin began his working life as a paper boy at the age of eight. Inspired by the songs he heard, he began singing in restaurants and bars as a teenager. By the time he was thirty, he was an established songwriter. As a lyricist and composer, Berlin "played a leading role in the evolution of the popular song from the early ragtime and jazz eras through the golden age of musicals."[84] He is best known for his musical *Annie Get Your Gun* and for his hundreds of classic hit songs, including "White Christmas," "Easter Parade," and "Cheek to Cheek." When the United States entered World War II, Irving performed and popularized the song he wrote years ear-

---

82 https://en.wikiquote.org/wiki/Albert_Einstein

83 "Irving Berlin," https://www.britannica.com.

84 https://www.britannica.com/biography/Irving-Berlin.

lier, "God Bless America," which became virtually a second national anthem.[85]

> Irving Berlin has no *place* in American
> music—he *is* American music.
> —Jerome Kern

Mark Rothko[86] (1903–1970) – his paintings are among the most recognizable of the twentieth century. He was born Markus Rothkowitz in Dvinsk, Russia. Rothko was ten years old when his family migrated to the United States in 1913, settling in Portland, Oregon. He attended Yale University from 1921 to 1923 but dropped out when his scholarship ceased and moved to New York. He is known as an abstract expressionist painter—a label he rejected—his early paintings were impressionistically figurative, in the tradition of Cezanne and Matisse. His abstract work began in the 1930s, and in the following decade, he became involved with the abstract expressionist artists called the New York School. For twenty years, he worked part-time as a children's art teacher at the Brooklyn Jewish Center. By 1940, he became an American citizen and shortened his name. His mature work of the 1950s and '60s displays his characteristic style of "soft-edged rectangles arranged vertically against a monochrome… background."[87] His work was influenced by mythology, Nietzsche, and Jewish and social revolutionary thought.[88]

> A painting is not a picture of an
> experience but is the experience.
> —Mark Rothko

---

[85] Nancy Churnin, *Irving Berlin: The Immigrant Boy Who Made America Sing* (New York-Philadelphia: Published by Creston Books, LLC, 2018).

[86] Mark Rothko, National Gallery of Art, https://www.nga.gov>features>markrothko.

[87] https://www.nga.gov/exhibitions/2023/mark-rothko-paintings-on-paper.html.

[88] Andy Tuohy, *A to Z Great Modern Artists* (New York: Octopus Publishing Group Ltd., 2015).

Hedy Lamarr[89] (1914–2000) – Hollywood legend and brilliant inventor. Hedwig Eva Maria Kiesler was born in Vienna, where, as a child, she was encouraged by her bank director to develop an interest in mechanical construction while her mother exposed her to lessons in piano and ballet. At age sixteen, she studied acting. In 1937, she met Louis B. Mayer of MGM in London, which launched her Hollywood career.[90] She starred in films for the big screen, such as *White Cargo* and *Samson and Delilah*, and also appeared on television.

When she met the eccentric business tycoon Howard Hughes, he mentored her inventive interests by "giving her a small set of equipment to use in her trailer on set." By studying the characteristics of the fastest fish and birds, she designed a new type of airplane wing for Hughes, who called her a "genius."

During World War II, Lamarr collaborated with writer-composer George Antheil to come up with a way to obstruct German military operations. This experimentation resulted in their development of the frequency hopping technology that has made possible "today's Wi-Fi, GPS, and Bluetooth communication systems."[91] In 2014, Hedy Lamarr was posthumously "inducted into the National Inventors Hall of Fame."

> People seem to think because I have a pretty
> face, I'm stupid. I have to work twice as
> hard as anyone else to convince people I
> have something resembling a brain.
>
> —Hedy Lamarr

Leonard Bernstein[92] (1918–1990) – world-renowned conductor and composer. Influenced partly by the liturgical music he heard during his youth at his family's temple, Mishkan Tefila; by twentieth-century composers, including Aaron Copeland (whom he

---

[89] Richard Rhodes, *Hedy's Folly: The Life and Breakthrough Inventions of Hedy Lamarr, the Most Beautiful Woman in the World.*

[90] https://www.womenshistory.org/education-resources/biographies/hedy-lamarr#.

[91] https://www.womenshistory.org/education-resources/biographies/hedy-lamarr#.

[92] Leonard Bernstein, https://en.m.wikipedia.org/wiki/Leonard

befriended while at Harvard) and Gershwin; and by jazz and popular music[93]—it is not surprising that Bernstein developed a marvelous capacity to blend classical with popular genres of musical presentation. He grew up in Massachusetts, one of three children of Jewish immigrant parents from Russia. He was the first American-born conductor to achieve international recognition and developed an iconic reputation for his achievements, the best known of which is his creation of the music for West Side Story—in collaboration with choreographer Jerome Robbins and lyricist Stephen Sondheim.[94]

He conducted the New York Philharmonic Orchestra, and his Young People's Concerts with that orchestra were televised.[95] He was involved for many years at the Tanglewood Music Center, where he taught and mentored students.[96] He especially enjoyed introducing children to the joys of classical music, as well as inspiring the general public to a greater appreciation for music. Moreover, he guest conducted many of the world's leading orchestras and had special associations with the Vienna Philharmonic[97] and the Israel Philharmonic. "In 1947, Bernstein conducted in Tel Aviv…with the Israel Philharmonic Orchestra, then known as the Palestine Symphony Orchestra."[98] He loved the works of Gustav Mahler and helped to retrieve respect for his works.

In addition to composing orchestral music, Bernstein wrote chamber music, choral works, and piano pieces. He also created music for theater (*On the Town*), ballet (*Fancy Free* in 1944, *Dybbuk* in 1975), opera (*Candide*), and film (*On the Waterfront*). Moreover, he and his wife Felicia were lifelong political activists and participated in promoting civil rights and world peace and raising "money for HIV/AIDS research and awareness."[99] In 1989, "Bernstein conducted the historic *Berlin Celebration Concerts* on both sides of the

---

[93] https://grammymuseum.org/museum-at-home/revisit-leonard-bernstein-at-100/
[94] https://grammymuseum.org/museum-at-home/revisit-leonard-bernstein-at-100/
[95] https://grammymuseum.org/museum-at-home/revisit-leonard-bernstein-at-100/
[96] https://www.bso.org/stories/bernstein-at-tanglewood-a-love-letter.
[97] https://leonardbernstein.com/about
[98] https://en.wikipedia.org/wiki/Leonard_Bernstein
[99] https://en.wikipedia.org/wiki/Leonard_Bernstein

Berlin Wall while it was being torn down."[100] At one point in the biopic film *Maestro*, Bradley Cooper, as Lenny Bernstein, expresses his concern about the smallness of his legacy; in fact, his wide stylistic variety of numerous compositions, the enormous collection of his recordings (that include lectures as well as musical performances), and his impressive list of notable awards (Grammys, Emmys, Tonys, and Kennedy Center Honor) all up to a very distinguished musical legacy for the ages.

> This will be our reply to violence:
> To make music more intensely, more
> beautifully, more devotedly than ever before.
> —Leonard Bernstein

Stan Lee[101] (1922–2018) – creator of iconic superheroes. Stanley Martin Lieber was born in New York to Romanian-born Jewish immigrant parents. Lee made comic book history. He began his career as a teenager. He introduced hero after hero. He is the man behind the beloved characters, The Incredible Hulk, Spider-Man, the Fantastic Four, Thor, the X-Men, and many more. After decades of writing and editing, Lee broke into writing for movies and television through his company POW! Entertainment.[102]

> There is only one who is all powerful,
> and his greatest weapon is love.
> —Stan Lee

Jerry Lewis[103] (1926–2017) – the king of comedy. He made his mark on the public arena as a consummate entertainer—an American comedian, a sentimental clown, a Hollywood movie star, a Vegas icon, a singer, a film producer, a screenwriter, and a tireless

---

[100] https://leonardbernstein.com/about

[101] 101. "Stan Lee," https://en.m.wikipedia.org/wiki/Sta

[102] 102. Stan Lee, Peter David, and Colleen Doran, *Amazing Fantastic Incredible* (New York: Touchstone an imprint of Simon & Schuster Inc., 2015)

[103] 103. "Jerry Lewis," https://en.m.wikipedia.org.

philanthropist. His inimitable comic style made him a star performer and a household name during the 1950s and '60s. He conducted telethons that earned millions for muscular dystrophy research and treatment. When he became national chairman of the Muscular Dystrophy Association in 1956, Lewis dedicated his time to the cause, for which he received several accolades, including the Jean Hersholt Humanitarian Award.[104]

> Adrenaline is wonderful. It covers pain. It
> covers dementia. It covers everything.
> —Jerry Lewis

Elie Wiesel[105] (1928–2016) – internationally acclaimed author and champion of human rights, a Holocaust survivor. Recipient of the 1986 Nobel Peace Prize, Wiesel made it his life's work to bear witness to the genocide committed by the Nazis during World War II. He was born in Romania to Yiddish-speaking parents with a rabbinic heritage. Of the fifty-seven books he has authored, his memoir *Night*, based on his incarceration at the age of fifteen in the concentration camps at Auschwitz and Buchenwald, is his best-known work. After his liberation, he studied at Sorbonne and then became a journalist. He moved to the United States in 1955 and subsequently taught at Toston University, Yale, Columbia, and other leading universities. He cofounded Moment Magazine in 1975, and he helped establish the United States Holocaust Memorial Museum, which opened in 1993. Through his public speaking, his books, and his political activism, Wiesel was instrumental in bringing the Holocaust—also called *the Shoah* ("calamity" in Hebrew)—to world consciousness. He actively protested against Holocaust deniers and spoke out against oppression worldwide.[106]

---

[104] Shawn Levy, *King of Comedy: The Life and Art of Jerry Lewis* (New York: St. Martin's Press, 1996).

[105] "Elie Wiesel," https://en.m.wikipedia.org>wiki.

[106] Linda Bayer, *Elie Wiesel: Spokesman for Remembrance (Holocaust Biographies)* (New York: The Rosen Publishing Group Inc. 2000).

> We must always take sides. Neutrality
> helps the oppressor, never the victim.
> Silence encourages the tormentor,
> never the tormented.
>
> —Ellie Wiesel

Stephen Sondheim[107] (1930–2021) – redefined the Broadway musical form with his innovative and award-winning productions. He was born into a Jewish family in New York. His paternal grandparents were German Jews, and his maternal grandparents were Lithuanian Jews from Vilnius. He studied piano and organ, and at age fifteen, he wrote a musical at George School in Bucks County, Pennsylvania. At this time, he was mentored by a neighbor who happened to be Oscar *Hammerstein II. Early in his career, he wrote the lyrics for West Side Story*[108] *and Gypsy.* He then went on to write both the music and the lyrics for subsequent productions, among them *A Funny Thing Happened on the Way to the Forum* (which, incidentally, featured Jewish actor Zero Mostel). He is known for the remarkable range of musicals he wrote and composed, from *West Side Story* to *Sweeney Todd* to *Into the Woods.*[109] Sondheim enlisted the help of Lin-Manuel Miranda in translating *West Side Story* into a Spanish production for stage, after which he offered Miranda some advice on creating *Hamilton.* His best-known song, of the hundreds he wrote, is "Send in the Clowns," popularized by Judy Collins. Sondheim is regarded as a major innovator of twentieth-century musical theater.[110]

> If I cannot fly, let me sing.
>
> —Stephen Sondheim

---

[107] "Stephen Sondheim,".

[108] "West Side Story," Wikipedia,

[109] DT Max, *Finale: Late Interviews with Stephen Sondheim* (New York: HarperCollins Publisher, 2022).

[110] DT Max, *Finale: Late Interviews with Stephen Sondheim* (New York: HarperCollins Publisher, 2022).

Joan Ruth Bader Ginsburg[111] (1933–2020) – RBG was a force to be reckoned with…who broke gender barriers and stood up for women's rights. She was born in Brooklyn, New York. Her father was an immigrant from Odesa, Ukraine, which was part of the Russian Empire at that time. Her mother was born in New York to Jewish parents who came from Krakow, Poland, which was part of Austria-Hungary at that time. In school, Ruth played the cello, was a member of the honor society, and was a baton twirler. Sadly, her mother died of cancer the day before Ruth's graduation from James Madison High School. In 1954, she graduated from Cornel and married Martin Ginsberg. Two years later, she enrolled at Harvard Law School, where "Ginsberg took on the challenge of [helping] her sick husband…with his studies while maintaining her own position at the top of her class."[112] She was the first woman in the Harvard Law Review, and in 1959, she completed Columbia Law School no less than first in her class. Another first was her becoming the first tenured female professor at Columbia in 1972.

Having experienced salary discrimination as a female working in law offices together with the academic slights she received from the male establishment as a student in the 1970s, she led the Women's Rights Project of the American Civil Liberties Union. There she challenged "gender discrimination and successfully argued six landmark cases before the US Supreme Court. In 1980, Ginsberg was appointed to the District of Columbia's US Court of Appeals."

At the time of her appointment by President Clinton in 1993, when she was sixty years old, Ginsberg was the second woman and the first Jewish woman ever appointed to the US Supreme Court. At that time, the courthouse did not have a women's bathroom for justices until Ruth pointed it out. Ginsburg's continued fight for women's rights was evident when she championed and won the case for admitting women to the Virginia Military Institute in 1996.

RBG, as she fondly came to be called, had an exceptional attendance record while serving as a Supreme Court justice, even while

---

[111] "Joan Ruth Bader Ginsburg," https://www.oyez.org>justice>Ruth Bader Ginsburg.
[112] "Joan Ruth Bader Ginsburg," https://www.oyez.org>justices>Ruthbaderginsburg.

being treated for cancer at the end of her life. She was eighty-seven years old when she passed and had gone through multiple battles with cancer and a heart operation.[113] Ginsburg's most famous quoted words express her characteristically Judaic *tikkun olam* philosophy:

> To make life a little better for people
> less fortunate than you,
> That's what I think a meaningful life is.
> One lives not just for oneself
> but for one's community.
> —Joan Ruth Bader Ginsburg

Gloria Marie Steinem[114] (born 1934) – journalist and activist leader in the Women's Liberation Movement. The late 1960s to the early '70s is known as the decade of second-wave feminism. Together with other leading feminists, Gloria Steinem made her mark as an outspoken activist for women's equality. Her iconic good looks contributed to making her a media superstar—which, unfortunately, at times deflected attention away from her political voice. Through the organizations she helped to found—the National Women's Political Caucus, the Women's Action Alliance, and the Women's Media Center—she worked collaboratively with feminist leaders with women journalists, legislators, and other activists to advance women's rights, such as equal pay for equal work. She advocated for the Equal Rights Amendment, reproductive freedom (an expression she coined, meaning the choice to have or not have children), and civil rights. She protested against the Vietnam War and South African apartheid.

She was a columnist for *New York* magazine. In 1971, Steinem cofounded the publication *Ms. Magazine.* In a 1979 *Ms. Magazine* article, she brought to public attention the global issue of female mutilation. She helped establish *Take Our Daughters to Work Day.*[115]

---

[113] Kathleen Krull and Nancy Zhang, *No Truth without Ruth: The Life of Ruth Bader Ginsburg* (New York HarperCollins Publishers, 2018)

[114] "Gloria Steinem," https://awpc.cattcenter.iastate.edu

[115] Carolyn Daffron, *Gloria Steinem* (New York-Philadelphia: Chelsea House Publishers, 1988).

In recent years, Steinem has spoken out in support of same-sex mar-riage and LGBTQ rights.

> Empathy is the most radical
> of human emotions.
> — Gloria Steinem

Chapter 10

Interviews

DL Lang
Vallejo Poet Laureate (2017–2019)

What is your biggest challenge in your field as a layperson?

I minored in Judaic studies in college, and at one time, I wanted to be a rabbi and had the honor of leading morning prayers at my synagogue. I am not as active in the community as I used to be due to ill health, so perhaps my biggest challenge is that due to my physical disabilities for the past decade, I have been unable to fully participate in Jewish life, but thankfully, I have the ability to memorize the prayers and songs, and I belong to a welcoming congregation that has embraced me. Judaism has informed my poetry and inspired a great deal of it over the years, and I wouldn't be a spoken word performer were it not for the encouragement of the lay musicians.

How would you explain Jews are "the chosen people?"

"Chosen" just means an obligation to follow the 613 *mitzvot* (commandments), which is something that non-Jewish folks are not at all obligated to do. These religious laws are just a way of connecting to the divine. Judaism believes all righteous people have a place in the world to come, and that includes people of other religions, atheists, and of no religion. The goal of Judaism is to make the world a better place for all people, not just Jewish folks. All religions have their specific guidelines for adherents to follow. I do not interpret chosenness as Judaism being superior to any other culture or faith.

In my case, although I am not as religious or active as I used to be, in my twenties, I chose to follow Reform Judaism because it made the most sense to me after studying about world religions. Reform allows room for modern interpretation, personal choice, and disagreement. For other people, their spiritual calling may be more in line with other faiths or another branch of Judaism, and in my opinion, all faiths and cultures have beautiful traditions within them. Unfortunately, we all have our zealots who use religious texts to justify carrying out harmful actions in the name of whatever "-ism" that runs counter to pluralism and universalism.

Why do you think Jews are constantly attacked?

Going back to Genesis, our belief is all people are made in the image of God, and racism and bigotry are a sin because you are attacking God's creation. We are commanded to pursue justice and love the stranger. Because of that belief, people like Rabbi Abraham Joshua Herschel marched with Dr. Martin Luther King Jr., and many Jews are currently engaged in modern social justice movements as well. People like White supremacists who are against progress for racial and religious minorities tend to put all the blame on Jewish activists rather than seeing progressive movements as a multicultural coalition of people working together for the common good.

Interreligious bigotry won't go away until fundamentalism is abolished, and a more humanistic approach to religion and tradition is globally adopted to prevent zealotry. Christian supersessionism (believing that Christianity abolishes Judaism) and Islamist beliefs about killing infidels certainly play into why the Jewish people are attacked in majority Christian and Muslim nations. The violence doesn't start with bombs, guns, or knives—it starts with ideas and language. If we had mandatory comparative religion and culture classes where every student would learn about every faith and pagan folk customs, it would help to reprogram the culture away from anti-Semitism, Islamophobia, and other hatreds.

Human beings are unfortunately very susceptible to propaganda, and rather than spend years studying in college courses about a religion, they take the easy way out and just believe the lies propagated by people who were not Jewish and often had no contact with Jewish folks. The poison of anti-Semitism predates Hitler, who merely synthesized old hatreds, drawing inspiration from people like Henry Ford, the historical ghettoization of Jewish people by the Roman Catholic and Ottoman empires, and how America treated Black and indigenous people. Hitler, unfortunately, had collaborators in world leaders such as the Haj Amin Al-Husseini, the mufti of Mandatory Palestine, and Pope Pius XII, which perpetuated the bigotry far beyond the borders of Germany—and this history continues to have an effect on modern times. Anti-Semitic rhetoric continues to morph and is fueled by ignorance and institutions that have something to gain by othering the Jewish people.

Anti-Semitism is contradictory: Both do not want Jewish people to be in the Diaspora and do not want Jewish people in their historical homeland; both blame Jewish people for the inequalities within capitalism and for the failures of the Soviet Union, completely ignoring the historical realities and atmosphere that Gentiles have created, such as only allowing Jewish folks to work in moneylending because of Christian prohibitions and then being bigoted toward Jewish folks for being competent at doing so, or carrying out violent pogroms and passing laws that expel Jewish folks from European or Muslim countries and then being equally angry when Jewish folks decide to go back to their biblical homeland.

Hatred is completely illogical and just finds a way to blindly criticize without being grounded in reality. The idea that Jewish folks, a mere 0.2 percent of the population, control the world is completely laughable. If this were the case, the average Gentile would be able to name far more Jewish holidays than just Hanukkah, and we'd all be getting several extra weeks of paid time off instead of having to worry about losing our jobs to comply with observing Shabbat (Saturday Sabbath) and other holidays that require ceasing our day-to-day labor. As to the modern-day conflict in Israel and Palestine, I don't claim to have any answers, but it is going to take compromise and level-headed leadership on both sides to cease the violence and find a solution where both peoples can coexist in peace.

Where do you see the Jewish culture and religion in the future?

Judaism has survived for centuries, and I think it will continue to evolve and adapt to whatever modern life brings. It is much more than a religion—it is a peoplehood, and a belief in God is not required to be Jewish. There are many secular Jewish folks who still practice some traditions to stay connected. Jewish culture has inherent positive values of working to make this world better for all humanity, whether there is an afterlife or not (*tikkun olam*), volunteering labor, and giving money to causes (*tzedakah*).

What message about the Jewish people do you want to send to those who will be reading this book?

Get to know the Jewish people instead of just reading what others have written about us. You will largely find a group of warm, welcoming, loving, and kind people. If Columbus was a crypto-Jew or his crew were Jews expelled in 1492, as some have said, then there is also a moral reckoning to be had about our role in the maltreatment of indigenous peoples in the Americas, and having some indigenous ancestry, I'm personally not a fan of Columbus's actions for that very reason.

~~~~~

Alex Cabeza
Moreh/Teacher

Please describe your career.

The faith-based communities of all religions require teachers and workers who are trained and dedicated in their respective functions in order to sustain and strengthen the continuity of their respective movements. My particular faith is most commonly known
~~~~~

as Messianic Judaism, which is founded on the Hebrew Scriptures with a focus on the person and teachings of Yeshua, whom Gentiles refer to as Jesus. Although, like all faith movements, there are a variety of views on what the Messianic faith is, we all agree that our goal is to live a biblical lifestyle based on all of Scripture.

This distinguishes us from mainstream Judaism and Christianity for the following reasons. Mainstream Judaism prioritizes rabbinical interpretations of Scripture, which is given more time and attention than the Hebrew Scriptures. Even more so for Christianity, the majority of the Hebrew Scriptures are rejected by all Christians in regard to actual application and are replaced with church decrees and interpretations. For example, Christians reject the biblical life cycle and holy days and only refer to the Old Testament for historical or philosophical purposes. Most Christians reject the Sabbath and holy days, which were all observed by not only Yeshua but all of his original disciples for the first few generations. My career as a Messianic instructor/teacher (*moreh*) is to return to the teachings and lifestyle that were practiced by Yeshua and his original followers.

What is your ministry?

My particular ministry includes teaching under the authority of Rabbi Itzhak Shapira, Rabbi Avner Ben-Yehuda, and Rabbi Emanuel Goffman, all of whom are Jewish disciples of Yeshua Messiah (Christ). This means I teach on their respective platforms and communities. The focus of the teachings is centered on the weekly readings of the Torah, Genesis-Deuteronomy, and how to apply them—as individuals, families, and as a community that believes in Yeshua as the Messiah sent from the God of Israel to empower us in our covenant relationship with the Creator.

I also have a personal ministry, Outcasts of Israel, which focuses on the restoration of the "Marranos/Anusim," which are the descendants of Jewish believers forced to reject the Hebrew Scriptures and forced to submit to the Romanized version invented by Constantine in CE/AD 325. We also do outreach for prisoners and people involved in the "street" lifestyle—the literal outcasts of society. Our goal is to lead them to the God of Israel through the works and teachings of Yeshua the Nazarene.

What motivated you to become a rabbi?

The term rabbi is a controversial term in the movement for many reasons. In the first century, it was used to refer to a teacher of the Hebrew Scriptures. After the destruction of the second Jewish temple, the term was strictly used by someone ordained by the successors of the Pharisaic branch of Judaism. Previously, there were several branches of Judaism or the Israelite faith. For example, Essenes, also known as the "doers" or the "sons of light;" there were also the Sadducees; there were also the Samaritans; there were subgroups of Zealots; there were also Jewish Hellenistic movements that sought to incorporate Jewish beliefs with the Greco-Roman culture; and of course, the dominant branch, the Pharisees from whom the later rabbis come from.

Aside from that, someone's Jewish status is taken into account. For example, I have one Jewish grandfather and my other grandfather descends from the Marranos/Anusim, who were the Jewish Catholics of Spain, Italy, and Portugal. I am accepted by my Jewish leaders, but not all Messianics are of one common position on who is accepted as Jewish. For that reason, I prefer the term moreh, which means a teacher or instructor in the general sense.

What is your biggest challenge trying to recruit Messianic Jews?

The biggest challenges are the complete unawareness of modern Christians in regard to the murder and torture of Messianic and non-Messianic Jews by the Roman Catholic Church. From the third century, and even before, all the way to the fifteenth century, there was no other denomination in the western Christian world. When a man named Martin Luther led a movement to separate from the Roman church, he retained all anti-Jewish beliefs and even wrote about burning down all synagogues, Hebrew Scriptures, and even Jewish people. He is the founder of all modern Christian Protestant denominations in the Americas. The wicked Hitler used his writings to implement his plan to murder all Jews in the name of Christianity.

Of course, Christians in America and Britain rejected this wickedness, but they were left with the task of separating themselves from over a thousand years of European Christianity that endorsed this behavior. Many Christians in America began to review the Hebrew Scriptures anew and concluded that the Jewish people are still, indeed, God's people, but many American Christians simply ignored this history. The reason this history is largely suppressed is because the question is then asked: If the Jewish people are still God's people, then where does that leave Christians? This is a problem for the Jewish community because they cannot ignore 1,700 years of Christian hate, and it is an identity crisis for Christians. That is what the Messianic movement seeks to resolve in our generation—answering how both Jewish people and true biblical Christians are both a part of God's people.

How would you explain Jews are "the chosen people?"

In Acts 1:6–7, the Apostles of Yeshua, whom he himself left in charge of his movement, asked the following: "Therefore, when they had come together, they asked Him, saying, 'Master, will You at this time restore the Kingdom to Israel?' And He said to them, 'It is not for you to know times or seasons which the Father has put in His own authority.'"

In this statement, the apostles make no mention of restoring the kingdom to a new "church." What's more compelling is that Yeshua does not correct them and say, "That's done with," or "Now there is a new church." Yeshua acknowledges that the kingdom will be restored to Israel by simply stating that the Father knows that time. In other words, the Father will accomplish the restoration of Israel in his time. One can also read literally any single book of the Prophets, and they all speak of the restoration of the kingdom of Israel and their people. Every prophecy is focused on restoring not only the people of Israel but also the land. During the generation of Yeshua, the land was occupied by the Romans and their proxies, the Sadducees and Herodians.

Why do you think Jews are constantly attacked?

The Jewish people are always attacked simply because they are God's people. For example, Christians would hunt them down for practicing any aspect of the Mosaic Law during the Inquisitions. Islam was established under the foundation of the Roman church, replacement theology, which teaches that God replaces his people if they are disobedient in some way. That means in order for the church or Islam to be God's "true" people, they somehow have to deal with the existence of the Jewish community—the actual writers of the original Bible and people of Scripture.

Where do you see Jewish culture and religion in the future?

When the Messiah Yeshua returns, he will not establish a universal church. He will restore the kingdom to Israel, and he will allow all his followers from the nations to join his people, depending on whether they truly followed his teachings or the teachings of man-made religion.

What message about the Jewish people do you want to send to those who will be reading this book?

They are the chosen priests of God called to lead all humanity back to the Creator. All of Yeshua's apostles were Jewish, so this process has already begun, but the final stage needs to be completed, the "fullness of the Gentiles:" Romans 11:25, Genesis 48:19, Ephesians 4:17, and Ezekiel 37—all of which state that a remnant from every nation will unify with the Jewish people to worship the God of Israel under the leadership of Yeshua the Messiah.

~ ~ ~ ~ ~

Brenden Lafferty
Bible Teacher
Christian School

Please describe your career and ministry.

My career and my ministry are tied together. I am a Bible teacher. I consider my teaching position as my current ministry. In January 2023, after preaching at the school's chapel, I was approached by the high school Bible teacher and asked if I had ever considered being a teacher. I humorously told him that I had never thought about it. Up until that point, I had planned to go into marketing after I graduated from university. I graduated with a marketing degree. My plan was to work in marketing or sales for two or three years, save money, and then move to Los Angeles to attend seminary. As the months went by, the thought of being a Bible teacher began to grow on me, and I reached back out to the school. The application process soon began afterward. I had no idea God would put me into a ministry position so soon. I get to teach the Word of God to young men. I cannot imagine a better job.

What is your biggest challenge in your teaching role?

There are a few challenges as a teacher, but for me personally, I would have to say it is remaining patient and discerning what I do and do not have time for. I have to remain focused and patient in the midst of interruptions and talking during our class time. Some days are more challenging to be slow to anger and frustration than other days. I see those days as God's means of sanctifying me—which, in the end, is for my good (Romans 8:28). I have not been a teacher for long, but I have noticed a difference in my level of patience. The other pressing challenge I face is deciding what to talk about and what not to talk about. The problem does not lie in that I am purposely withholding God's Word in any way—the challenge lies in how much I want to say and only having fifty minutes to say it, all the while having to accomplish other classwork.

How would you explain Jews are "the chosen people?"

Beginning in Genesis 12, God chose Abram (later Abraham) to be a great nation. Now the Lord said to Abram, "Go forth from your country, and from your relatives and from your father's house, to the land which I will show you; And I will make you a great nation, And I will bless you, and make your name great; And so, you shall be a blessing; And I will bless those who bless you, And the one who curses you I will curse. And in you all the families of the earth will be blessed" (Genesis 12:1–3 NASB95). Abraham and Sarah eventually conceived and bore Isaac. And Isaac and his wife later bore Jacob. Jacob wrestled with God, and God blessed him, and Jacob's name became Israel (Genesis 32:24–32). Israel had twelve sons, which became the twelve tribes of Israel. Through the rest of Scripture, we see God's unfolding plan of redemption, salvation, and blessing with the nation of Israel. King David would later be raised up, and from his line, the Messiah, King Jesus, would eventually come (reference Matthew 1:1–17, Luke 3:23–38).

Why do you think Jews are constantly attacked?

There are two ways of answering this question. One, it is because men hate each other. Since man's fall into sin (Genesis 3), men have been hostile with one another ever since (Genesis 4) and continue to this very day. The second way of answering the question as to why Jews are constantly attacked is because they are the chosen people of God. Because of sin, man's natural condition is rebellious and hostile toward God. In Romans 8:6–8, the apostle Paul says, "For the mind set on the flesh is death, but the mind set on the Spirit is life and peace, because the mind set on the flesh is hostile toward God; for it does not subject itself to the law of God, for it is not even able to do so, and those who are in the flesh cannot please God." The unregenerate mind, which is man's natural condition, "is hostile toward God." If man is naturally hostile toward God, they are going to be hostile toward not only him but to one another and toward God's chosen people. All throughout the Old Testament, we see nations warring against and oppressing Israel—and that sadly has not changed.

Where do you see the Jewish culture and religion in the future?

I cannot tell you what the culture and Judaism will look like in the near future. But one thing I can tell you is that God highly exalted him and bestowed on him the name which is above every name, so that at the name of Jesus *every knee will bow*, of those who are in heaven and on earth and under the earth, and that every tongue will confess that Jesus Christ is Lord, to the glory of God the Father (Philippians 2:9–11NASB95).

What message about the Jewish people do you want to send to those who will be reading this book?

We must pray for the salvation of lost souls, Jews, and Gentiles.

~~~~~
~~~~~

Chapter 11

Keywords

Anti-Semitism – hostility to or prejudice against Jewish people.

Ashkenazi – (adj.) originally used to refer to Jews who lived in western Germany as early as the tenth century; nowadays, describing those Jews who are descendants of families from Eastern and Central Europe—in other words, the Jews who are not considered Sephardi (Ashkenazim = noun). https://hms.harvard.edu>news

Bigotry – a refusal to let go of a prejudicial view of an idea; prejudice toward a person solely because of their being a member of a certain group. Racism and anti-Semitism are forms of bigotry.

Canaan – Canaan was the name of a large and prosperous ancient country (at times independent, at times a tributary to Egypt) located in the Levant region of present-day Lebanon, Syria, Jordan, and Israel. It was also known as Phoenicia.

D-Day – On June 6, 1944, the Allied powers launched a massive attack against the Nazis on the coast of Normandy in France that was intended to end the war. It did, in fact, cause a turning point in the war that culminated in the German surrender the following year.

Diaspora – a word of Greek origin that means "to sow over, or to scatter." Thucydides, the ancient Greek historian, used the word for the scattering of the Greek population to describe the Greeks' dispersal. Later, the word was applied to describe the forced exile, in the sixth century BCE, of the Jews during the Babylonian conquest.

Fascism – a dictatorial type of governmental rule over a society where it is unlawful to express criticism of the rulers.

Government in Israel – Israel is a republic with a president as head of state and a prime minister who runs the executive branch, balanced by the judiciary and the Knesset (the name of Israel's parliament), located in Jerusalem. https://embassies.gov.il>Pages>Isr

Hitler – "Adolf Hitler is one of the most well-known—and reviled—figures in history. As the leader of Nazi Germany, he orchestrated both World War II and the Holocaust, events that led to the deaths of at least 40,000,000 people."
https://www.britannica.com/list/9-things-you-might-not-know-about-adolf-hitler

Hebrew – Modern Hebrew is the official language spoken in Israel, while Hebrew in its ancient and pre-modern forms is used for liturgy or Talmudic study. "Biblical scholars use the term Hebrews to designate the descendants of the patriarchs of the Hebrew Bible…Abraham, Isaac, and Jacob (Genesis 32:28)—from that period until their conquest of Canaan (Palestine) in the late second millennium BCE."

Holocaust – The World War II genocide of European Jews by Nazi Germany that, together with collaborating nations and individuals, systematically murdered six million men, women, and children, amounting to two-thirds of European Jewry.

Israelite(s) – the people described in the Hebrew Bible as the "descendants of any of the sons of the patriarch Jacob (later called Israel)."

Jew – "a member of the Semitic people who claim descent from the ancient Hebrew people of Israel…and are linked by cultural or religious ties." Also, a "person whose religion is Judaism."

Judaism – "a monotheistic faith affirming that God is one, the creator of the world and everything in it. Judaism had its beginnings some 3,800 years ago in Mesopotamia…with Abraham, the founding patriarch of the tribes of Israel."

Knesset – the parliament of Israel in Jerusalem.

Messianic Jews – Jews and Christians who believe that Jesus Christ is the Messiah and who actively proselytize in order to increase their following.

Moreh – The Hebrew word (*moreh*) is "one who throws." This can be a teacher (or father) who throws (points) his finger in a direction the student (or son) is to take. It can also be an archer who throws an arrow at a target.

Moses – He is known as the quintessential "prophet in Judaism and one of the most important prophets in Christianity, Islam, the Druze faith, the Bahá'í faith, and other Abrahamic religions." In the Bible and in the Koran, Moses was the leader of the Israelites and lawgiver [credited with] the authorship, or acquisition from heaven, of the Torah.

Netanyahu, Benjamin – "Bibi" Netanyahu is the current prime minister of Israel who has served in that office a total of sixteen years over three non-successive terms, beginning in 1996. This makes him the longest-serving person to hold that office. He also happens to be the first prime minister born in Israel since the birth of the state.

Orthodox Judaism – Orthodox Judaism is the collective term for the traditionalist branches of contemporary Judaism. Theologically, it is chiefly defined regarding the Torah, both written and oral, as revealed by God to Moses on Mount Sinai and faithfully transmitted ever since. Orthodox Judaism, therefore, advocates a strict observance of Jewish law, or *halakha,* which is to be interpreted and determined exclusively according to traditional methods and in adherence to the continuum of received precedent through the ages. It regards the entire *halakhic* system as ultimately grounded in immutable revelation, essentially beyond external influence. Key practices are observing the Sabbath, eating kosher, and Torah study. Key doctrines include a future Messiah who will restore Jewish practice by building the temple in Jerusalem and gathering all the Jews to Israel, belief in a future bodily resurrection of the dead, and divine reward and punishment for the righteous and the sinners. "Orthodox Judaism" – news ▫ newspapers ▫ books ▫ scholar ▫ JSTOR (August 2021).

Prejudice – "preconceived opinion that is not based on reason or actual experience…[such as] *prejudice* against people from different backgrounds."

President of Israel – (2023) Isaac "Bougie" Herzog is the eleventh president of Israel. He began his term in 2021. He is the first of eleven presidents born in Israel since its independence.

Racism – prejudice, discrimination, or antagonism by an individual, community, or institution against a person or people on the basis of their membership in a particular racial or ethnic group, typically one that is a minority or marginalized. The belief that different races possess distinct characteristics, abilities, or qualities, especially so as to distinguish them as inferior or superior to one another. "Theories of racism" definition from Oxford Language (Wikipedia) https://en.m.wikipedia.org>wiki

Sephardic – (adj.) the Jews of Spain, Ladino, also known as Sephardi Jews or Sephardim, and seldom as Iberian Peninsula Jews, are a Jewish diaspora population associated with the Iberian Peninsula (Spain and Portugal). The term, which is derived from the Hebrew Sepharad (Spain), can also refer to the Jews of the Middle East and North Africa, who were also heavily influenced by Sephardic law and customs. Many Iberian Jewish exiled families also later sought refuge in those Jewish communities, resulting in ethnic and cultural integration with those communities over the span of many centuries. (Sephardim = noun) Latino, Hispanic, or Sephardic? A Sephardi Jew explains some commonly confused terms by Sarah Aroeste/December 13, 2018.

Synagogue – The term synagogue is of Greek origin (*synagein: to bring together*) and means *a place of assembly*. The Yiddish word *shul* (from German *Schule*, "school") is also used to refer to the synagogue, and in modern times, the word *temple* is common among some Reform and Conservative congregations. https://www.britannica.com>topic

Torah – In Judaism, Torah is the law of God as revealed to Moses and recorded in the first five books of the Hebrew Scriptures (the Pentateuch).
Definitions from Oxford Languages

Xenophobia – Dislike of or prejudice against people from other countries.
Definition from Oxford Languages dictionary

Zion – The scripture refers to Zion as the "City of Holiness" and a "city of refuge" where the Lord protects his people from the evils in the world. It is also used among Christian groups to mean "utopia."
Zion – definition, meaning & synonyms/Vocabulary.com

Zionism – a movement for (originally) the reestablishment and (now) the development and protection of a Jewish nation in what is now Israel. It was established as a political organization in 1897 under Theodor Herzl and was later led by Chaim Weizmann.
Definition from Oxford Languages dictionary

Epilogue

A Remarkable Odyssey

The struggles of the Jewish people to endure and survive throughout history have been endless and filled with tears. Our civilization is trapped by so many biases that can be compared to chains. Yet we have the potential and capability to overcome and grow a new outlook. Perceptiveness is dynamic; morality is dynamic; history is dynamic; society is dynamic; ideas are dynamic. Intangible things—such as religion, morality, and ideologies—have dynamic value through the ages. Initially, the culture of masters and slaves was admissible. By the twentieth century, a change had evolved: All human beings are born free; therefore, there are no masters and slaves. Even though the political philosopher Jean-Jacques Rousseau, in one of his most important works of political theory on inequality, *The Social Contract,* in 1755, his opening line is still striking today and is still unresolved: "Man is born free, and everywhere he is in chains." Rousseau agreed with John Locke, an English philosopher and physician, that "the individual should never be forced to give up his or her natural rights to a king."[116]

Many of us have left our respective countries of birth, but we will always carry the aroma of our origins. While in our journey as immigrants or descendants of immigrants, and, for that matter, everyone, let us raise our voices for the voiceless. Let us raise awareness to stop this dark human cruelty that victimizes our fellow human beings. Why

---

[116] John Locke, "The Second Treatise on Civil Government," (1689), https://www.norton.com>documents.

did it take until December 1941 for the United States to finally join the Allies against Germany in World War II, which had been raging in Europe and Asia for more than two years? This is an under-discussed issue of which the West will always be criticized for its inactivity.

No matter what the daily routine is, the secret of our future is hidden in our daily activities. Let's not forget to include empathy—compassion, appreciation, help to other people, and our lives will be happier and more fulfilling. Albert Einstein said, "Humanity is going to require a substantially new way of thinking if it is to survive."

Unfortunately, greed is an insatiable desire for material gain or social value, such as status or power. Happiness and wealth are believed to walk side by side. Are all wealthy people happier? No, they are not. Greed starts with the desire for something little, next something bigger, more…more…and more. The biblical figure Cain murdered his brother, the shepherd Abel, because he was enraged when the Lord accepted Abel's offering in preference to his own. Israel, another biblical figure, son of Jacob and Rachel, loved Joseph more than any of his other sons because Joseph had been born to him in his old age. Yet Joseph's brothers hated him. They seized him and sold him into slavery.

In 1939, Hitler, an aggressive, egocentric, and cruel-minded dictator, occupied Czechoslovakia. The excuse for this act was the foreign exchange crisis. Germany decided to seize the gold of the Czechoslovak Central Bank. This was an act of pure greed. The opposite of greed is what the world is asking for—generosity, benevolence, and love.

The United States of America represents the American dream. Do migrants and refugees find what they are looking for in "the land of milk and honey?" Many of them are treated harshly and inhumanely. According to Professor of Psychology Dacher Joseph Keltner, "We are wired up to compete, especially in Western society, and that creates separation."

What are the lessons learned? The central characters in this book are the Jewish people. This book is about people who have spread or been dispersed from their homeland. Their story is about unity and family, as well as strong spiritual beliefs and moral values. I believe that Judaic culture represents a profound poem of courage touched by deep sadness. This narrative covers ancestry, religion, culture, and more. Judaism is the story of people who have used faith, hope, and courage to dream and overcome adversity. We can find inspiration in the diary of a sensitive young girl, Anne Frank, with an extraordinary optimism and hunger for knowledge while she was in hiding for two years with her family during the Nazi occupation of the Netherlands.

We can gain knowledge while meeting people from different races, religions, and cultures—who can introduce us to different cuisines and new ways of thinking. In a country such as the United States that is religiously, culturally, and ethnically diverse, it is important to respect other religions and cultures. This is a supportive society that respects and tolerates differences. Choices and taking risks can be life-changing, and every individual should have the freedom to make their own decisions.

In order to understand a culture, one must not judge its conditions according to the precepts of our own culture. Each person should adopt customs that might enrich their life and discard those that might not agree with their ethical standards. Every individual should decide for themself and not let anyone else decide for them. Another factor is that when we are born, we don't select our parents, our race, our religion, our political position, or our country of birth. However, as we grow up, it is our decision to decide about who we want to be. No one should be blamed, and no one should blame others.

The Lutheran theologian Reinhold Niebuhr is best known for his Christian Realism, which emphasized the persistent roots of evil in human life. In his *Moral Man and Immoral Society* (1932), he stressed the egoism and the pride and hypocrisy of nations and classes. These words of prayer are attributed to Niebuhr (1892–1971):

> God, grant me the serenity to accept the things I cannot change, the courage to change the things I can, and the wisdom to know the difference.[117]

---

[117] Reinhold Niebuhr, "Prayer for Serenity," Marquette University, https://www.marquette.edu>faith.

Throughout his life, Niebuhr cultivated a good reputation and rapport with the Jewish community. He was an early critic of anti-Semitism in Christianity and was also a persistent critic of Nazism and rising anti-Semitism in Germany throughout the 1930s. He famously said, "Love is the motive, but justice is the instrument."

Let Us Raise Our Voice

Let us shout praises to Yahweh
In the sunlight
In the moonlight
In the darkness
Let us speak love
We are to love others
As we love ourselves
Let us shout of joy
And the wall of tribulation will fall down
Let us raise awareness
We can be quiet and show our identity
We can speak up and hide our identity
Many times, even if we don't say a word
People can figure it out
The world needs our love and our generosity
Let us raise our voice for the voiceless
—Ilean Baltodano

Despite everything, I believe that
people are really good at heart.
—Anne Frank

Acknowledgments

I owe it all to my mother for her love, energy, strong work ethic, resourcefulness that drove her entrepreneurial spirit and, above all, for her vision for me to learn English without knowing I was going to move to the United States of America. To my father who made a profound influence on my writing. He inspired me by raising his voice for the voiceless through his publications and poems. To my five daughters, who are a gift and a reward from heaven, and to my husband, who departed too soon.

I am much obliged to the Writer's Workshop in Benicia, California. They participated in the production of this book by reading and editing early drafts. The experience and support of this team were essential. Thank you also to my editor, Alyza Lee Salomon, for her incredible talent. You made my book so interesting and clear.

I could not have written this book without the support of the Benicia Public Library. When the library didn't have what I needed, the staff obtained the materials by contacting other public or university libraries.

Thank you to those who were kind enough to give me the opportunity to interview them.

I am sending special gratitude to those who believed in this effort and encouraged me: DL Lang, Vallejo Poet Laureate (2017–2019); Mary Susan Gast, Benicia Poet Laureate (2021–2023); Phil Canalin, member of the Benicia Writers Workshop; and members of the Benicia Library Poetry Salon.

Bibliography

Books

Alper, Ann Fitzpatrick. *Forgotten Voyager: The Story of Amerigo Vespucci.* Minneapolis: Carolrhoda Books, 1991.

Anne Frank House. *Anti-Semitism: Past and Present.* Translated from the Dutch by Lorraine T. Miller. 2016 Anne Frank Stichting, Amsterdam. The Netherlands, Publication Boom, 2005.

Barasch, Marc Ian. *Field Notes on the Compassionate Life: A Search for the Soul of Kindness.* Pennsylvania: Rodale, 2005.

Barry, Dave, Adam Mansbach, and Alan Zweibel. *A Field Guide to the Jewish People.* New York: Flatiron Books, 2019.

Bayer, Linda. *Elie Wiesel: Spokesman for Remembrance (Holocaust Biographies).* New York: The Rosen Publishing Group Inc., 2000.

Bornstein, Michael and Debbie Bornstein Holinstat. *Survivors Club: The True Story of a Very Young Prisoner of Auschwitz.* New York: Farrar Straus Giroux Books for Young Readers. An imprint of Macmillan Publishing Group, LLC.

Churnin, Nancy. *Irving Berlin: The Immigrant Boy Who Made America Sing.* New York-Philadelphia: Published by Creston Books, LLC, 2018.

Daffron, Carolyn. *Gloria Steinem*. New York-Philadelphia: Chelsea House Publishers, 1988.

Friedman, Tova and Malcolm Brabant. *The Daughter of Auschwitz. My Story of Resilience, Survival, and Hope.* Toronto, Ontario: Hanover Square Press, 2022.

Fuson, Robert H. *The Log of Christopher Columbus*. Camden, Maine: International Marine Publishing Company, 1987.

Hallo, William, David Ruderman, and Michael Stanislawski. *Heritage: Civilization and the Jews. Study Guide.* New York: Praeger Publishers, Educational Broadcasting Corporation, 1984.

Heinrichs, Ann. *Gerardus Mercator—Father of Modern Mapmaking.* Minneapolis, Minnesota: Compass Point Books, 2008.

Hurowitz, Richard. *In the Garden of the Righteous: The Heroes Who Risked Their Lives to Save Jews during the Holocaust.* New York: HarperCollins Publisher, 2023.

Keneally, Thomas. *Schindler's Ark.* Great Britain: Serpentine Publishing Co. Pty. Ltd., 1982.

King, Ross. *Artists Their Lives and Works.* DK London: Penguin Random House, 2017.

Krull, Kathleen and Nancy Zhang. *No Truth without Ruth: The Life of Ruth Bader Ginsburg.* New York: HarperCollins Publishers, 2018.

Laikin Elkin, Judith. *Jews of the Latin American Republics.* North Carolina: The University of North Carolina Press-Chapel Hill, 1980.

Lee, Stan, Peter David, and Doran, Colleen. *Amazing Fantastic Incredible*. New York: Touchstone an imprint of Simon & Schuster Inc., 2015.

Levy, Shawn. *King of Comedy: The Life and Art of Jerry Lewis*. New York: St. Martin's Press, 1996.

Lowing, Joseph. *Heritage: Civilization and the Jews, Viewer's Guide*. The Brookdale Foundation, Educational Broadcasting Corporation, 1984.

Mann, Charles C. *1491: New Revelations of the Americas before Columbus*. New York: Published by Alfred A. Knopf, 2015.

Max, D. T. *Finale: Late Interviews with Stephen Sondheim*. New York: An Imprint of HarperCollins Publishers, 2022.

Mooyaart-Doubleday (translated from the Dutch). With an introduction by Eleanor Roosevelt. *Anne Frank: The Diary of a Young Girl*. New York: Batam Books, 1993.

New International Version, *The Bible*. Zondervan, 1973.

Parker, Steve. *Albert Einstein and Relativity*. New York-Philadelphia: Chelsea House Publishers, 1995.

Potok, Chaim. *The Chosen*. New York: Ballantine Books, 1967.

Pieper, Liam. *The Toy Maker*. Australia: Penguin Random House, 2016.

Prager, Dennis and Joseph Telushkin. *The Nine Questions People Ask about Judaism*. New York: Published by Simon and Schuster, 1981.

Roth, Philip. *Goodbye, Columbus*. New York: Vintage Books, a Division of Random House Inc. 1993.

Sale, Kirkpatrick. *The Conquest of Paradise: Christopher Columbus and the Columbian Legacy*. New York: Published by Alfred A. Knopf Inc., 1906.

Silverman, Emily Leah. *Religious Visionaries in the Time of the Death Camps: Edith Stein and Regina Jonas*. Durham: Acumen Publishing Limited, 2013.

Stein, Edith. *The Classics of Western Spirituality: Selected Writings*. New York: Published by Paulist Press, 2016.

Stein, Lori and Ronald H. Isaacs. *Let's Eat: Jewish Food and Faith*. Maryland: Published by Rowman & Littlefield, 2016.

Steinbacher, Sybille. *Auschwitz: A History*. Translated by Shaun Whiteside, 2005. New York: HarperCollins Publishers Inc.

The Jewish Publication Society of America. *The Torah, the Five Books of Moses*. A new translation of the Holy Scriptures according to the traditional Hebrew text. Philadelphia, Pennsylvania, 1967.

Thomas, Gordon. *The Pope's Jews: The Vatican's Secret Plan to Save Jews from the Nazis*. New York: Thomas Dunne Books-St. Martin's Press, 2012.

Timerman, Jacobo. *Prisoner without a Name, Cell without a Number*. New York: MacMillan Publishing Co. Inc., 1981. This book is a translation of *Preso sin Nombre, Celda sin Número*.

Tuohy, Andy. *A to Z Great Modern Artists*. New York: Octopus Publishing Group Ltd., 2015.

Vaughan, Marcia (author) and Ron Mazellan (illustrator). *The Story of World War II Hero: Irena Sendler.* New York: Lee & Low Books Inc., 2011.

Wiesel, Elie. *Night.* New York: Hill and Wang—a Division of Farrar, Straus and Giroux, 2006.

Wiesenthal, Simon. *Sails of Hope: The Secret Mission of Christopher Columbus.* New York: MacMillan Publishing Co. Inc., 1973.

Wikipedia – online encyclopedia created and edited by volunteers around the world and hosted by the Wikimedia Foundation.

Articles/Papers/Websites/DVDs

Altman, Neil. "Humiliation, Retaliation, and Violence." American Journal of Psychiatry 146, No. 1–1989.

Eban, Abba. *Heritage: Civilization and the Jews. A Nine-Part Series on Three DVDs and One CD-ROM.*
> Volume 1: *A People Is Born / The Power of the Word / The Shaping of Traditions*
> Volume 2: *The Crucible of Europe / The Search for Deliverance / Roads from the Ghetto*
> Volume 3: *The Golden Land / Out of the Ashes / Into the Future*
> Volume 4: *Heritage Interactive* (CD-ROM)

Harrison, John Kent. *The Chronicle of the Courageous Heart of Irena Sendler.* DVD, 1998.

Kohn, Alfie. "Beyond Selfishness." Psychology Today. October, 1998.

Levy, Daniel S. "The Diary Endures: Anne Frank: Her Life and Her Legacy." *LIFE Magazine*, 2022 edition – a reissue of a special edition. pp. 1–96. Display: Until 8/18/2023.

Spielberg, Steven, director. *Schindler's List.* NBC Universal, DVD, 1993.

About the Author

Ilean Baltodano is the author of three previous books. Several of her recent poems have appeared in her local newspaper. She holds a master of science degree in human resources and organizational development from the University of San Francisco. She is a naturalized US citizen who immigrated from Nicaragua in 1979. After a career working in human resources for a major energy supplier, she is now happily retired and thriving in her multiple roles as a grandmother, writer, community volunteer, and global traveler. She enjoys playing the piano. Through her travel adventures, she educates herself about the value of connecting with the global community. Through her writing and her YouTube channel, she advocates against the injustices in Nicaragua, humanity, and Mother Earth. She lives in Northern California.

Books by Ilean Baltodano:

- *Still on Vacation* (2017)
- *Still on Vacation: In the Middle of a Pandemic* – Revised (2019)
- *Todavía de Vacaciones: En Medio de la Pandemia* (2020) (Spanish translation)

www.ingramcontent.com/pod-product-compliance
Lightning Source LLC
Chambersburg PA
CBHW021228130726
47988CB00002B/867